MW00436899

HEALING
the Invisible Wounds of
TRAUMA

HEALING
the Invisible Wounds of
TRAUMA

A Columbine Survivor's Story

KRISTEN KRUEGER

ILLUMIFY MEDIA GLOBAL
Littleton, Colorado

HEALING
the Invisible Wounds of
TRAUMA

Published by
Illumify Media Global
www.IllumifyMedia.com
"Write. Market. Publish. *SELL!*"

Library of Congress Control Number: 2018967791

Paperback ISBN: 978-1-949021-21-9
eBook ISBN: 978-1-949021-22-6

Printed in the United States of America

*To everyone who has ever survived trauma
and found themselves questioning why*

CONTENTS

PREFACE

This is my story. My experience as a Columbine High School shooting survivor. My story about walking through the impalpable depths of darkness, pain, and suffering. My story of waking up and breathing in new life. My story of healing and hope. My story of freedom.

That day in my life is forever cemented into my mind. Very little about it escapes my memory, as far as what was in my tunnel vision at the time. Everyone says that eyewitness testimony is sketchy, that it can change and morph over time. For some people, maybe.

However, I remember specific details echoed by my classmates over the few months and years following the shooting. Details such as the reality that the outside doors I and so many others ran through to escape the gunfire were in front of two closed fire doors inside the hallway, completely separating us from the end of the school where the "two" shooters were. That, even though, according to the official report, the two acknowledged shooters were at the opposite end of the school *behind* the two closed fire doors.

The truth is, I looked back and saw a third shooter, whom I and many others identified to law enforcement.

No matter how many times I and countless others detailed the name and descriptions of that third shooter—who wasn't even *supposed* to be at school that day—no one believed us.

One of the most traumatic aftershocks of that day was the knowledge that law enforcement ignored the warnings, ignored the signs hanging in the windows, and that countless other students who survived know that at least one other person was out for our blood that day. He still roams free because the easy answer is that Eric Harris and Dylan Klebold were the only shooters. After all, they were dead, and the weapons used were found by their bodies.

Only those of us that were there that day and those who knew what was happening and who participated in the shootings or helped to orchestrate the massacre know and speak out about this truth. The shooters were my friends. We were all the outcasts in that school, bullied because we didn't fit the mold. I knew Eric and Dylan, I also knew the third shooter, which explains why I was able to clearly identify him to law enforcement. That fall semester before the shootings occurred, all my red flags were raised with this group of friends. They were obsessed with death and revenge and were clearly unstable. Although I wasn't the most emotionally healthy person at that time, I knew the difference between right and wrong, and refused to participate in their "fantasies." For this reason I intentionally distanced myself from that group during that fall semester and never looked back.

Strength and healing require perseverance. You cannot move forward if you constantly look back. Knowing what I do about what really happened that day, about the frustration of trying to find someone, anyone, to believe you, is why I wanted to share my journey.

One of my favorite quotes on strength and pressing on comes from Winnie the Pooh: "You are Stronger than you seem, braver than you believe, and smarter than you think you are." Many people survive horrific pain and suffering but find themselves struggling to regain their footing. Many influences will tell you that you are weak, that you didn't suffer as much as someone else, that you should have gotten over it by now. I am writing this book to dispel and destroy those lies, regardless of where they originate. Strength, bravery, and intelligence are by-products of standing in the flames and refusing to succumb to the darkness that threatens to destroy you. The strongest, bravest, and smartest people I've ever known are the ones who ask for help, who admit their own weakness, and who fight to find the light and reclaim the life that was stolen from them.

This book is dedicated to everyone who has ever survived trauma and found themselves questioning why. Why do I still suffer? When will this pain ever end? Why me? I pray that you find hope, support, and strength in what I say. You are not alone. Never give up the fight to reclaim your life. It's worth it. I promise.

INTRODUCTION

If you had told me twenty years ago that I would have survived one of the worst mass school shootings in United States history, I would have told you that you were deranged. I never would have imagined a world where a book like this would exist, let alone that it would be based on my life experiences instead of a work of fantasy. I always believed that evil existed in this world, but I never expected evil to come knocking at my door. The truth that the horrific actions of a few would leave me broken and bleeding for decades after the fact was something that never crossed my mind. I was young; I was naïve; and every structure of safety, identity, and understanding of this world and of who I am was utterly destroyed in the matter of minutes.

Now, twenty years and innumerous horrendous acts of terrorism, mass shootings, wars, and ravages of childhood trauma later, there is still so much that is misunderstood and distorted regarding how survivors respond to these events. Due to a dearth of misinformation and ignorance, we've seen a rise in substance abuse and addictions, increases in major psychiatric diagnoses, and an epidemic of veterans and active duty military members—twenty-

1

two *every* day!—so despondent that they choose suicide over dealing with their invisible wounds.

Statistics tell us that in 2017, 103 firefighters and 140 police officers committed suicide. In 2009, studies demonstrated that correctional officers committed suicide at twice the rate of other law enforcement professionals. This doesn't include the number of children under the age of eighteen who commit suicide annually as a result of bullying and other abuses, a symptom of this society that breeds hopelessness. What's worse is this number has been increasing steadily over the last decade. Every year, an estimated 44,965 people die by their own hand in the United States!

What explains the growing epidemic of suicide, substance abuse, and debilitating mental illnesses that is ravaging our children, families, friends, and coworkers? This world is constantly being subjected to the evil schemes of people who willingly hurt others for no other reason than because they want to. Amidst the constant excuses and debates between professionals about what drives perpetrators to act, no one wants to admit that these things happen because people *choose* to hurt others. The rates of Adverse Childhood Experiences (ACE), mass traumas, and repeated traumas has escalated and become more sensationalized. Conversely, the rates of Posttraumatic Stress Disorder (PTSD), depression, anxiety, and other mental health diagnoses have also increased. The incidence of PTSD diagnoses in children is jumping at alarming rates as well.

These realities speak volumes about the indelible stigma associated with the normal responses to surviving trauma. I hope to bridge the gap between what professionals and talking heads want you to believe and the truth about surviving trauma and the subsequent reactions to these events. With my own experience of surviving multiple traumas before the age of eighteen, I knew even then, that unless something changed, people like me would forever be classified as *broken*.

In 1999, few professionals understood PTSD, and the ones I encountered offered disconnected, competing, and conflicting ideas about how survivors should present themselves and how to treat the resulting symptoms. It became painfully clear to me as I was shuffled, drugged, and labeled that no one in the psychiatric or medical field knew what was going on, and most didn't really care to find out. As a result, I was forced to advocate for my own care, identify my own diagnoses, and understand my own experience and symptoms. At this time, professionals only accepted symptoms that followed exactly the course described as they interpreted it. I, as does every other survivor, did not have all the symptoms at the same time. Some symptoms were obscured, and others were delayed in expressing themselves. As a result, my need to advocate for myself was seen as being difficult, rather than the truth that I knew myself and was demanding that the "professionals" do their jobs.

As you read this book, I hope you will be able to breathe a sigh of relief. That you will be able to begin understanding that what you survived created the chaos in your life. And that your symptoms, struggles, and concerns are *normal* not pathological. Expecting people who have survived hell to pick up the next day and continue as if nothing happened is ignorant and dangerous. This book will help you navigate what's going on inside your mind, your body, your relationships, and everything else impacted by the traumas you endured.

> *Your symptoms, struggles, and concerns are normal, not pathological.*

First, I want to help you understand what trauma looks like when you experience it. The entangled, confusing, contradictory thoughts, feelings, and behaviors encompassing your trauma demonstrate that there is no one way a person experiences it. What you suffered and how you reacted will likely differ greatly from someone else experiencing the same event. That is normal. The belief that everyone should respond to trauma the same way is wrong, and numerous scientific studies now confirm this.

Following this initial look into trauma, I begin to address different ways that trauma can impact your life. Surviving trauma leaves permanent changes in the structure of your brain, the structure and prevalence of the chemicals and hormones in your mind and body, which will impact your ability to function at work and in relationships. No one can escape the ravages inflicted on trauma survivors. You will wrestle with struggles, concerns, and dysfunction in multiple areas of your life as you begin to understand what you endured and begin putting the pieces of your soul back together. However, the struggles, pain, and chaos you are experiencing are not permanent, or at least they don't have to be. PTSD does not get better on its own. Time alone does not heal these wounds. You can, however, with qualified professional help, heal from them and learn how to create and embrace your new normal.

Trauma destroys your sense of safety and your identity—who you thought you were and how you perceived the world, other people, and most importantly yourself. This is normal. Many people are able to quickly heal from trauma and resiliently adapt to life after the event(s). If you aren't one of those people, that doesn't mean something is wrong with you. Research is beginning to show that access to a healthy and strong support system and the ability to find a safe place to process your experience are crucial to healing, but even some who have access to that level of support can still suffer with PTSD. If you did not have access to such support, realize that it's not a function of who you are, your strength, your intelligence, or any other part of you to place blame for "not being able to get over it."

It is, however, a function of who you have in your life, the environment you return to, and the culture of the environment in which you survived your trauma. The environments for military members, law enforcement, and first responders are notoriously poor in providing a safe place to admit that you're not okay after whatever hell you were exposed to. This is likely the main reason for the prevalence of suicide, substance abuse, and psychiatric disorders in these communities.

When you are faced with a hostile environment where it is unsafe to admit your struggle or that doing so would result in the loss of your job, expect to have difficulty recovering. I learned that no one would ever be able to adequately advocate for me. I needed to figure out how to fight for myself, advocate for my own care, and not let anyone convince me of what I knew to be wrong. It is exhausting fighting for someone to listen to you, but when you emerge from the darkness, when you are finally able to breathe in the fresh air of freedom from the chains of trauma, the battle will have been worth it.

Suffering immeasurable pain and surviving horrific trauma changes your life. You will never be able to return to your former life, which isn't all bad. Your strength and power will come from being able to transform your pain and become someone stronger than you could ever imagine. Learning how to find meaning and purpose in your life after trauma is one of the most powerful ways to transform your pain into power. You will find, as you persevere through the healing journey, that you discover your true self, your true identity, one that includes the past but does not allow the past to control and define you.

The journey to healing is hard—sometimes excruciatingly hard—but it is the most important battle you will ever face, and the one that will have the most impact when you emerge victorious and free.

1

JUST LIKE THAT . . .
EVERYTHING CHANGES

A moment changes everything. A moment.
—David Gray

BOOM!
What was that? What's going on? Why is someone lighting off fireworks?

BOOM, BOOM, BOOM!!

Those aren't fireworks, those are gunshots! We have to get out of here!

I can barely breathe as I sprint to the front doors, knowing instinctually that I must get away from the gunshots or I will die. I've been around guns my whole life, I know what can happen when someone chooses to use that weapon as a tool of destruction. I know that no matter what, I have to break free from the building. That I must run and not stop for anything.

What do you do when, in one moment, your entire existence is destroyed, your identity shattered, and your safety stripped from you, and you now must figure out how to survive and thrive in the pain and chaos of what just happened? How do you start over and heal?

***

"Mommy Made Me Mash My M&Ms," is being sung in the choir room. Warm-ups are finally beginning as we try and settle in for my favorite class. I love choir, I love singing, and music. Something about sound and music brings joy and hope into my soul. *I love this one*, I think, *because I get to play with my vocal range and sing high and low notes I wouldn't normally get to as an alto.* I always like to push my voice, and as my senior year is coming to a close, I enjoy knowing I was able to participate in the audition-based All-State Choir competition this year. I feel confident in my voice and delight in the monotony of the vocal gymnastics.

That's weird, I wonder. *Why is he showing up so late again? It's so distracting! Oh well, he's always coming in late.*

"Mommy made me mash my—"

That sounds like gunshots! It must be fireworks. That's an interesting senior prank. Someone's going to get in trouble. Why do people think it's funny to do that kind of stuff?

"We've got to go! Someone is shooting up the cafeteria," one of my classmates yelled as he stood next to the keyboard, clearly panicking.

"What are you talking about? Get in your seat, let's go."

"No! Listen, get out of here!"

Then we all make the connection: It's not fireworks; it really *is* gunshots. Instantly, and in total confusion, I am up and running out the east door of the classroom. Pushing through the narrow doorway and into the hall leading to the auditorium.

Are they getting closer? Why are the fire alarms going off? Is there a fire too? What is going on?

I'm in full survival mode now, and I am vaguely aware that I am not thinking, just doing. As the tunnel vision closes over my mind, all I can see is a path across the auditorium and out the other door into the hallway. As I cross the top of the auditorium, I hear a resurgence of gunfire as the shooters shoot up the cafeteria. I am following no one in particular; I am not even aware of who I am running with. As I exit the door that leads me to the front of the school, I realize that the only way out is the front door. The fire doors in the hallway separating the front of the school from the back of the school, where the gunshots are ringing out, are fully closed and sealed. We all have to go out the front of the school.

As we turned to go back to the front of the building, we run past a student just standing there. *Huh, I wonder what he's doing there in that hallway,* I think. *Why is he just standing there? Is that a gun?*

When I get close to the front of the school and the doors that lead us to safety I hear an audible voice in my head loudly order *"DUCK!"* I have no reason not to comply, so I crouch and run.

Boom! Crash!

A bullet grazes the top of my head as it shatters the glass of the door I'm pushing to exit the school. I have no idea what is going on, but I slam into the door and feel an ache in my arm and keep running.

Who's shooting at me? I thought they were at the other end of the school in the cafeteria, and the fire doors are shut! It's him; he's part of this; he's not just watching from the hall!"

When it was all over, I realized that the person who I saw point a gun at us, was not one of the two identified shooters. He wasn't even a student at Columbine anymore; he dropped out. *He isn't even supposed to be here!* yet here he was, trying to kill us all.

"What's going on? Where is everyone going?" a teacher called out. I am vaguely aware of a teacher entering the school in the opposite direction as the wave of students sprinting out.

"Someone is shooting at us!" I yell like this should be the most obvious thing and keep running.

"Can I borrow your phone?" I shout as I grab it from someone running beside me, not waiting for an answer. I call my mom at work.

"Mom, they're shooting at us, and I don't know where Eric is!" Then I drop the phone and run.

Somehow my mom is able to pick me up and drive me home, where my brother is waiting for us. He should have been in the cafeteria, but he came home for lunch. I lived across the street from the school at that time, and when I got home, my brother was in the park behind our house with hundreds of other students "watching" what was happening.

Later he told me how close he could have been to dying. He was an athlete (their supposed targets), a kind athlete, but an athlete nonetheless. As he walked home from school, he passed by their vehicle and saw them inside preparing for their rampage.

As shots continued to ring out, students begin pouring into our backyard seeking shelter and safety from the mayhem. It still isn't over, and it lasts well beyond the accepted fifteen minutes of active shooting narrative that became the official statement of record.

For the next few hours, hundreds of students gather in our home, borrowing our cell phones as they desperately try reaching their families. More than anything, I want to leave my neighborhood and go anywhere.

Where are they? They were right behind me! What happened?

I ponder these questions as I realize that my only two friends in the world didn't follow me out of the school. I realize the only answer is that they're still inside the school, or worse. Later in the day, I end up at the Jefferson County Public Library, adjacent to the school, one of the places where the students were being bussed. There, I numbly and desperately search for their names on the survivor's lists.

"I'm sorry, I don't know where she is. I thought she was right behind me," I replied as my best friend's dad frantically asked me where she was. *She should have been right next to me; we were only one seat apart!* Ultimately, my two best friends, the only people who helped me maintain any sense of self and normalcy during that horrible phase of my life, were still stuck in the school. Later I learned they had burrowed together with about thirty other of my classmates in a small, windowless room while the killers prowled the premises searching for new victims. My friends had to wait for law enforcement to finally arrive at their end of the school, where everyone else had perished. Despite the phone calls for help and signs hanging outside the windows from the school telling them the location of the survivors, my friends waited for hours.

Later that night, after buses stopped arriving from the school, I somehow managed to get from the library to Leawood Elementary School where my mom was waiting with her friend and the other twelve families, who by that time must have suspected their children were dead. To this day, one interaction haunts me and destroys me to my very core. I was wandering around, numb and dissociated from the trauma, when I ran into a desperate mom.

"Do you know where my son is? Have you seen him? No one knows where he is? What happened?"

"I don't know where he is, but I'm sure he's fine. He has to be. They'll find him soon."

It was Isaiah Shoels' mother. Of course, he wasn't fine. Law enforcement already knew where he was but had not officially notified his family yet. I didn't know her; I had no idea what I was saying to her. I just wanted to reassure her, and maybe myself, that everyone was okay. I still hadn't heard from my friends, and I think I was just willing them and everyone else to be alive—even though I think I knew that the thirteen families of those inside the school were not going to be taking their children and loved ones home that night. Years later, when I remembered this brief, yet poignant, conversation with Isaiah's mom, I was broken on a whole new level. To this day, I wish I could speak with her again and tell her I'm sorry. I know that I did nothing wrong, but I feel that in that moment I gave her false hope that was swiftly destroyed forever.

As evening fell I walked slowly back to my house, vaguely aware that nothing was going to be okay, and that I was forever changed. Children and a beloved teacher and coach had been slaughtered in their classrooms. The lives of thousands of students, teachers, administrators, and first responders had been altered forever . . . yet we had no idea the hell that was to follow our survival.

2

LIVING IN THE FLAMES OF A DIFFERENT HELL

There are wounds that never show on the body that are deeper and more hurtful than anything that bleeds.

—Laurell K Hamilton

Nothing in this life could have prepared me for what happened after surviving the Columbine High School Massacre—the deadliest school shooting in United States history at the time. Everyone knew the name Columbine, and they all reacted the same way when I told them where I went to high school: Either with extreme pity and horror or worse, excitement and gratitude at what the killers did to "make a point."

The next five years were a complete blur. I understand now my constant state of dissociation and fight/flight/ freeze mode, but I still struggled with the reality that five years of my life were mostly gone. I had jobs, met and interacted with people, and attended events of which I have no recollection. I spoke with victim advocates (one of whom I worked with later when I became a victim's advocate), investigators, and others who tried to piece together the chaos. I remember telling them what happened, what I saw, and whom I saw shooting at me, but they just nodded and dismissed my assertion that another person, a third person, tried to kill us. Of the few memories that remain from that time period, all that stand out are the negative ones. Anything positive is gone, and I am unsure of what, if anything, was positive in those moments anyway.

Almost twenty years later, I still look back on that day and struggle to remember more than what was in my tunnel of sight—I only remember what I try so hard to forget. The funny thing about trauma is that no matter how healthy you become, no matter how much healing you gain, those memories still pop up in unexpected moments and take your breath away.

The difference between healing and existing is that when those moments come, when your breath catches, when you feel your pulse quicken and the taste of bile rise in your throat, that is when people who have done their healing work are able to maintain themselves and stay in the present, or at least bring themselves back quickly. Those who have survived and are just existing every day have a much harder time bouncing back from those moments, and often find themselves in those moments, experiencing the nightmares and flashbacks more frequently because everything is still a strong trigger.

The farther removed I become from April 20, 1999, and the more I have pursued knowledge and understanding of trauma and how it compounds with each exposure to a traumatic event, the more I have been able to reflect on my life prior to that day. Columbine was the proverbial traumatic straw that broke this camel's back. This was not the first traumatic experience and it wouldn't be the last; however, it was the defining moment that changed me.

> *The difference between healing and existing is how you are able to stay present and not let those moments overtake you.*

The irony of the ever-destructive news media's conjecture regarding the motive of the killers was that they blamed horrific bullying for their decision to kill people. Yet, the innocent people who lost their lives weren't the bullies; they weren't even on their so-called kill list. To claim the killers suffered such a hard life that they felt homicidal rage as the only way to address their pain, enraged me. I knew they were mimicking the "party line," intentionally avoiding asking the hard questions, and that no one was really going to acknowledge their appalling act as pure evil.

I also knew how it felt to endure and survive horrific bullying. Years of torment and suffering at the hands of other people . . . yet I never felt the urge to do that.

The killers and their group of outcasts were friends of mine until the previous semester. Outcasts tend to gather together to try and create some form of belonging in an environment where they were relentlessly harassed. We ate breakfast together in the cafeteria until the behavior of many in that group became too bizarre, and they became obsessed with revenge, fantasy, and the live-action, first-person shooter video games. At that point, I decided to stop doing anything with them or our mutual "friends." I heard them complain, whine, and bad-mouth everyone they could. I vaguely remember their discussions about killing people, but I had no way to know what they were planning to do. And I certainly don't believe the bullying grew *so bad* that it became the catalyst for killing everyone they could.

Looking back, I have very few memories of belonging or even enjoying school, let alone life. I was relentlessly bullied from the time I started school, by both students and teachers, and it never got better. Recess became an exercise in avoidance and hiding, and more than once ended with me in the principal's office trying to explain what had just happened. Often, kids would chase me around the playground and taunt me, push me, hit me, or even throw rocks at me. During class, notes were passed, and hateful things were spoken outside of the hearing of the teachers. There was never a safe place for me at school. I never felt I could trust anyone other than a few select friends who were dealing with the same difficulties as me.

At that time, school administrators didn't deal with bullying like they claim to do now. Rather than taking bullying seriously, they tended to assume that any aggressive behavior was just kids being kids. These early experiences, without a doubt, distorted significant parts of my development and identity, but never did I ever experience a desire to act out like the shooters.

In first grade, I spent a significant amount of time during class in a corner behind a cardboard divider due to alleged "behavior," which my classmates and teachers were unable to articulate, but which was taken as the truth without my input. In third grade, as a result of early development, I was pulled into the girl's bathroom and forced to raise my shirt to show that, yes, they were real, which just changed the landscape of how that group of girls bullied me.

In fourth grade, my teacher took every opportunity available to bully me. One incident, where I was forced to defend myself against another classmate who stabbed me in the back with a pencil during class, I was again singled out and punished. This time, she locked me in a storage closet in the administration office for hours until my mom came to pick me up and no one could find me. This teacher was never admonished or punished yet continued to teach students until she retired. In sixth grade, when

I was (un)fortunate enough to hit puberty early, and I wasn't a skinny, pretty girl, life became almost unbearable at school. I was relentlessly bullied by both boys and girls for my size. I was never allowed to participate in their activities and was intentionally singled out by the popular kids as an especially favored target. In seventh grade, after being beat up by girls at the bus stop (the same girls who bullied me on the playground during recess in elementary school), never-ending taunting and teasing, even within my small group of friends, also outcasts, life became overwhelming.

Of course, I didn't really understand what was happening, but I knew that the excruciating emotional and physical pain had to be dealt with. No one taught me about self-harming; I just picked up a knife one day to "see what it felt like." I continued to cut until my twenties, when I finally realized the damage I was doing to myself. I grew tired of allowing the people who had tried to destroy me win. Only then could I break free from that specific destructive behavior.

My parents decided to take me out of the middle school I was attending at the time and enroll me in a charter school to try and protect me. It was a great idea, but the charter school was the absolutely worst school I could have attended. Not only was I already making destructive choices, but I was also physically assaulted by an angry ex-boyfriend when I was in eighth grade. At the school. In front of teachers. My guy friends who witnessed this eventually took care of the problem. Administrators did nothing. At all. And they even blamed me.

By this point, my life was on the downward spiral that culminated in the hell that was my high school experience after I returned to Columbine in tenth grade. Between eighth and eleventh grades, I was the victim of date rape by two different guys, self-harming, and told by a good friend that God doesn't exist—so nothing and no one could help me. Only by the grace of God did I survive high school without any lifelong addictions or permanently destructive behavior. God held onto me. He was the only One who saved my life.

I find it cathartic looking back at my life in light of the shootings to see how God took care of me and preserved me. Many events since then could have also resulted in my destruction, either physically or psychologically, yet God used them to redeem my pain and restore my vision of who I really was, instead of who I thought I was. He allowed me to heal in ways that I never would have thought possible, and in circumstances that should have been destructive.

Ten years after the Columbine massacre, I moved to the Washington, DC metro area to pursue a master's degree in forensic psychology. I was determined to help catch the predators that plague our world. Settling in to a life far away from home and loving what I was doing, I had an amazing best friend and a great group of friends from church. In this moment of new opportunities, I felt excited and hopeful about my life. As a survivor, I knew how to protect myself, to park under lights, never walk alone, and to walk with your keys like brass knuckles (DC doesn't allow any kind of weapon in the city limits). Before moving east, I trained in Krav Maga (the hand-to-hand combat technique used by the Israeli Mossad) and later appreciated the importance of continuing to be proactive in knowing how to defend myself.

On the evening of July 3, 2010, I walked to my car after attending an Independence Day event.

What is that?

Hearing someone running towards me, I began to turn around. That's when he grabbed me by my neck, put me in a chokehold, and tried to drag me away from my car. Somehow, even after a year had elapsed since actively training, my preparation kicked in, and I was able to move my neck enough to breathe and then proceeded to pummel him while he held on tight.

"Stop punching me or I'll kill you. I have a weapon!" he screamed at me as I punched, bit, scratched, and kicked everything within reach.

"No, you don't. If you did, you'd have already used it."

The rational conversation that was occurring while this guy was trying to kill me still astounds me to this day and demonstrates a profound difference in who I was and the healing I'd gained. After a few minutes, he finally decided to release me. He stood in front of my car, standing under the streetlamp at the train station where I had intentionally parked, just watching me.

"Get in your car and leave!"

"No! Not until you get away from me! HELP!" I yelled. "Call 911!"

Where are all the people that I was walking with? I thought.

"Hey, what's happening?" someone called out.

"Do you need help?"

No, I'm fine. This guy just tried to kill me. Of course I need help, idiot! Where have you been?

Then about a dozen people began calling 911 and chasing him away. Every single one of them was either too drunk to help or assumed he was my boyfriend or husband.

Why would it be OK for my boyfriend or husband to have his arms around my neck trying to kill me? What is wrong with these people? I thought.

After the ambulance and investigators showed up, and the adrenaline wore off, I realized that I wasn't terrified. I felt okay; empowered even. I sustained a pretty significant injury to my neck, but I was alive. The next day at a party, someone ran up behind me and I jumped. A moment of panic, but I didn't stay that way.

Hmm, I'm actually okay. I thought. *I should be freaking out right now, but I'm not. That's not the reaction I expected.*

I realized that although the enemy continued to try and kill me, as he had done many times in my past (most notably at Columbine), I had survived. Not only survived, but I was able to stand and fight to defend myself. I was thankful that my assailant attacked me and not one of the drunk women who were around me at the time, because I somehow knew he would have succeeded in his intention if he'd attacked anyone else but me that night. It's a bizarre thought to realize that this guy was going to try and rape and possibly kill someone that night, and because of my strength, intense healing work after the shootings, and my ability to defend myself and not get sucked back into my past traumas, God directed this guy's focus onto me. This prevented the enemy from succeeding in destroying lives that night, something that I have been trying to do since April 20, 1999.

Three years after surviving and defending myself against the attacker at the train station in Washington, DC, God used another horrific moment of trauma to allow me to again feel empowered and further the healing in my life, and hopefully the lives of others. I started dating a man (now my husband) whose oldest daughter was a student at Arapahoe High School during their 2013 school shooting. The extent of God's healing in my life became apparent in how this situation unfolded in our lives.

That morning at work, my phone rang.

It's Adam! I thought to myself as I looked at the screen. *I can't wait to talk to him.*

"Someone's shooting at her school. I have to get to her!"

"Wait, what? Okay, take a deep breath. We will get to her, do NOT go there without me. Get to my mom's house and wait for me to get to you!"

At that time, both Adam and I were federal law enforcement, and it was only because we had our federal law enforcement credentials with us, that we were able to get onto the school property while it was still an active scene and find his daughter safe. When the students began marching out of the school with their hands behind their heads, I felt myself re-experience the familiar sensations of trauma. God gave me an opportunity I didn't have at Columbine. I got to help.

3

THE NIGHTMARE BEGINS

Trauma is a fact of life. It does not, however, have to be a life sentence.

—Peter A. Levine

No one wakes up one morning expecting that their life will forever be changed. Each day brings new expectation and hope that things will turn out alright, that this day will bring a sense of peace and comfort. No one expects that their life is going to be turned upside down, that something no one thought possible is going to happen to them or around them. That's the chaos of trauma. It's sudden, unexpected, and violent. Even when the trauma suffered is continuous, as in the case of abuse or living in a war zone, a part of you hopes and believes that it will be different today. In a world where trauma, terror, and pain are continuously broadcast on the nightly news, you become desensitized to the violence in this world. Still, a part of you believes that those things happen to *other* people, not to you, and not to your loved ones.

That's how it was for me. I was raised to believe that evil exists, that there is a real enemy, Satan, whose whole purpose is to try and destroy everything and everyone that God created, and some people do horrible things simply because they want to. Multiple events in my life growing up validated this belief about the nature of humanity, and I began to seek out answers for how to survive in this world. I wanted to understand so I could keep my head above the water.

For a long time prior to the Columbine High School shooting, I had already experienced trauma and pain. I suffered in a way that no one could truly see or understand. I was the rebel, the loner, the one who always seemed to mess everything up. No one really knew, and I believed that even if they did, no one could understand the pain I was experiencing.

I believed the enemy's lie that if I told someone what was going on in my head, they would commit me to an institution, deeming me incurable for life.

You are really messed up. No one is ever going to want to have anything to do with you. No wonder you don't have any friends. Don't ever let anyone know the truth about what you're thinking!

One of the greatest lies the enemy perpetuates in someone's life is that there is no hope, no help, no healing.

That voice inside of your head that says, *You will never be free. You deserve to suffer. Nothing can make you right again.* Voices tell us no one will understand; we are all alone in dealing with the pain; and if we tell anyone, horrible things will happen to us or our loved ones. Predators use these same tactics to silence their victims. The silence of trauma and ongoing suffering following the trauma needs to be shattered. We need to believe that we are not alone, and that we do not need to hide and keep secret the torment going on in our lives.

Not much was different the morning of April 20, 1999.

"Why do I have to go to school? I hate this, I'm so glad I'm almost done with this!"

I woke up hating myself and hating the world, expecting another day of severe bullying, pain, and isolation. I didn't expect that day to be the final straw in the trauma of my life that would push me over the edge to dissociation and chaos, and the catalyst to change the course of my life from destruction to wholeness.

Truth is, I never expected much of anything to break the daily monotony and torment. Although the memories of my past were scattered and incomplete, they haunted my life. Even in that place, I had managed to create a pseudo-safe reality where I could try and keep the pieces together, where I could feel safe. In one moment, the small amount of safety that I felt was ripped from beneath me. I was breathless, devastated, and shattered.

The next five years, I barely existed in this life. I deeply believed this world was horrifically dangerous and that I was in someone's crosshairs every minute. I couldn't sleep and I forced myself to get through each day, just waiting until I could retreat to the seeming safety of my home. I realized that even though the shootings were the catalyst to the free fall into darkness in my life, the other things I experienced left permanent marks in my mind as well.

This distorted how I viewed the world, how I viewed myself, and how I viewed God. I realized that every relationship in my life, every self-destructive behavior, every overwhelming fear response to benign situations, was the result of my complex trauma reactions.

Then one day, I decided that enough was enough. I was tired of barely surviving, and that if I wanted anything different in this life, I needed to start living *my* life. After slowly self-destructing for years, I woke up one morning and realized that I wanted more than the destructive life I was living.

> The enemy's greatest lie is that there is no hope, no help, and no healing.

Our minds were created with the amazing ability to protect themselves from destruction. People's experiences before trauma and the patterns of beliefs and behaviors that develop in response to the traumatic events are unique to that person. This partly explains why no one really knows the best way to help someone who has been through hell. Because we are all individuals with unique abilities to learn and experience life, we must speak up for ourselves and tell others what we need in order to heal. Learning to identify and tell others what you need is a powerful step in the healing process. Acknowledging your weaknesses, allowing others to help you, and demanding effective treatment will be a strong catalyst that propels you through the healing process.

To heal from a painful and horrible past, you must find the courage to ask for help. I actively sought help from the beginning, before I even knew what was going on inside me. I trusted professionals to accurately and carefully evaluate what was happening in my world and give me the help I needed. But I quickly discovered that many people who claim to be professionals will ignore everything you say because it's easier to label you with a destructive and sometimes permanent diagnosis than truly uncover the cause of the distress.

During those five years after the shootings, I sought help from dozens of so-called professionals, none of whom were willing to look past the easy answer and tackle the difficulty in dealing with severe and persistent Complex Posttraumatic Stress Disorder (C-PTSD). I had all but given up at that point. I was overmedicated with drugs that did nothing to alleviate my symptoms nor treat the true cause of my psychological symptoms.

However, once I woke up and decided that enough was enough and that I wanted to live my life healthy and whole, I acknowledged that I couldn't heal on my own. The damage of my past was too devastating. I couldn't figure it out alone. This meant trying once again to find someone who would help me and not just slap me with some destructive and permanent label; someone who cared enough to help.

The amazing counselor who I started seeing after this realization once told me to "get busy living or get busy dying. You can't keep going like this and expect to get healthy."

This really incensed me. *How can you tell me that when I AM living, I'm doing the best I can?!*

"Everything I've experienced, all the trauma in my life has destroyed my sense of safety, of self-worth, and distorted my reality. You want me to just move on?!" I asked with exasperation.

"No, you have to make a choice about who you want to be. Either choose to live your life and heal or choose to wait until something or someone kills you."

I am the kind of strong-willed person who won't immediately admit that someone else is right—especially when they're really right. But the truth was that the diagnosis and medication were easy, they became crutches to stay unhealthy, to justify my destructive thinking. The drugs numbed me to how I really thought about my life and about others and about my behavior. The victim and C-PTSD label were furthering the destruction of my mind, body, and soul.

One fact still amazes me is that through everything, I never lost faith that God was real and that He was somehow involved in my life. I knew on an instinctual level that the *only* way I was alive and even remotely present and functioning was because God kept me tethered to Him. No matter how much I wanted everything to just stop, that I wanted to give up many times, He was not going to let go.

I was terrified to be stuck in the trauma cycle of psychological and emotional distress, so I began praying for someone to help me. Fortunately, God already had set those plans in motion; I just didn't know how they were going to play out. The counselor God lined up to help me through this trauma was someone I met ten years earlier when I babysat her children!

God knew what I was going to need to recover from the evils perpetrated against me and began putting things in place years before I needed it. That's the gracious and all-knowing power of God. We can never anticipate the direction of our lives, even if we're instinctually planners, but God can. He already knows what is in store for us, what we will struggle through and survive, and He begins the behind-the-scenes work needed. When we're finally ready and need that intervention, it is already waiting for us. He knows our greatest and most desperate need before we even know we have that need, and He waits for us to cry out to Him and ask.

When I began dealing with the effects of the shooting on my life, I recognized how many other smaller traumas were exaggerated by the shootings. This began my introduction to the concept of C-PTSD. As if one horror was not enough, many of us experience more than one trauma that should have and could have killed us.

At that time, I was barely holding onto the broken pieces of my life, but I was beginning to name and understand what lurked behind my suffering. Everything absolutely terrified me, and I did not even trust myself let alone trust anyone else in my sphere of existence.

As a result of my past experiences, I lost the ability to trust anyone except myself—and I trusted myself just enough to keep breathing. Realizing this gave me an opportunity to experience true healing, complete healing, rather than just trying to alleviate the symptoms that were disabling me. So often, we try to deal with the immediate issue, the most recent trauma, and ignore the effects of cumulative trauma—those other things that compound the negative effects trauma has on our lives. I quickly learned that since everything in my mind was so intricately entwined, I had a choice. I could deal with my past as a whole or settle for partial healing. I chose to dive in head first. If it was going to be painful, if it was going to hurt to deal with the shootings, I might as well deal with everything, so I could finally feel complete.

Now I am mostly free and healed from the pain of my past. The life I had and the life I had hoped for as a child cannot be recovered. I can never go back and undo what was done to me. Instead, I needed to redefine and learn how to thrive in the new normal. The lingering effects of the constant battle in my life are the negative thoughts and beliefs about myself and others that were created and cultivated through years of pain and trauma, and the lingering emotional struggles that seem to materialize out of nowhere. The difference is that now I am aware of those things and can actively work to heal those parts of my life when they come up. I am no longer blind to why I think and believe the way that I do, no longer unsure of where the pain and continuing struggles come from.

Before the shootings, I was already wandering in pain, just hoping that one day it would all end. The years of previous trauma and abuse had already taken their toll on me. Columbine just exacerbated everything and added new layers of suffering. For the first few years after the shootings I was the same way, just on a massively destructive scale. However, if not for the shootings, I may never have had the determination to get whole again. As I struggled and failed in my attempt to live life the way I wanted to, I may have never experienced the grace of God that I needed to be the person that I am today. The shootings were the beginning of the end of my struggle to survive this life and finally embrace myself despite my brokenness and become who I am today.

I wish no one would ever have to experience the pain of severe trauma and hurt, but I have a new understanding of the role those terrible experiences play in my life. Surviving hell allowed me to find strength in a way that I never knew possible. It allows me to be able to help people in a way that is intimately entwined in who I was created to be. I was always meant to help others, to be the light in the darkness, and to speak truth and help others fight for justice in every aspect of life. I would have been able to accomplish that without the trauma and pain in my past. But I don't believe I would be as effective and capable of fulfilling my calling if I hadn't experienced pain and tragedy in my own life.

I never wanted to experience so much pain in my life. I never really knew what kind of evil there was in this world. But every tear I have cried, every painful spasm in my body, and every broken piece of my heart and soul, God has cataloged and seen, and they will not go unused or unhealed. This is the true story of healing and redemption.

This world is desperately broken, and there are millions of people who are experiencing trauma and horrific acts of abuse and devastation in their lives every day. This world does not offer true hope. There is very little in this world that says that you can be free, that you can recover from what has happened. People are desperate for the truth, they are desperate for one moment of relief from the overwhelming pain they are experiencing. Those of us who have been through trauma, who have witnessed and experienced true evil and been able to heal and regain a sense of normalcy and peace in our lives, have a responsibility to speak hope and truth for the people who are still in the middle of their destruction, their devastation.

There is peace and tranquility in the middle of the chaos of life. There is hope for true healing and restoration of your life in Christ Jesus. He is the healer and the redeemer, and He has already defeated the enemy that desperately wants us to believe that there is no hope! The reality of the sacrifice and mercy of Christ is that we never walk through suffering alone.

The only way to find your way through the painful black of night is to cling to the true light.

I know this to be true, to be reality. Had it not been for the tangible presence of Christ in my life as I went through the deep darkness of trauma, I would not have made it out alive. I was on a path that would have inevitably led to my destruction, but God kept me from the more severe consequences I could not have endured. Had He not been guiding my life, I would not have been able to hold onto the truth that there is something beyond the pain. If I didn't know and believe that God is who He says He is on some level outside my consciousness, I never would have been able to make it to the other side of the immeasurable darkness.

This world was not created to be devastated and broken, but it is. The only way to find your way through the broken pieces and painful black of night is to cling to the true light, the only thing that makes sense in this life.

I cannot begin to understand why horrible things are allowed to happen, but I do know that no matter what, those events and circumstances are not ignored. They are not glossed over with God. He has a purpose for both good and bad for each and every one of us. Healing from your past allows you to find that meaning and purpose in a profound way that you may never have fully experienced without the trauma. Those of us who have experienced trauma are not alone. We are connected in a way that no one wants, but it is how we live with the events that connected us, is what truly defines us.

There is hope, there is healing, there is restoration, no matter where you are in your healing journey. Some may just be thinking about taking the step toward healing; others have been on this journey for a long time. No matter where you are the journey will get easier. You can thrive in this life, not just survive.

4

SUFFOCATING IN THE DARK

I survived because the fire that burned inside of me was brighter than the fire that burned around me.

—Joshua Graham

"Hey, are you ok? You look like you just saw a ghost.
"Oh, uh, yeah, I'm good. Just tired."

What is wrong with me? I have no idea what I just missed. I feel like I'm losing my mind! Well, maybe you are . . . it wouldn't be that far off to think you would crack after all this.

When you feel like you're losing your mind, you struggle identifying what is real and unreal. You wake up in the morning in a thick fog, trying to find your way to the light that seems to move further and further away, the more you try to reach out to grab it. You feel unsure of your surroundings, paranoid that everyone and everything is a threat, waiting to destroy what is left of your body and soul. The feeling is so intense, you're terrified of even breathing. This is exacerbated when you know at least one other person involved in your trauma who is still free, and you think that he will come after you.

The uncontrollable thoughts race in your head even when you know they are irrational and "crazy."

Okay, if I go to sleep now, I can get an hour of sleep before I need to get up and take my final . . . wait, did I even study for this test? What day is it? Crap, let me check my calendar again. Nice one, Kristen. Now you are really screwed. Do you even know what you did last night? I've got to get some sleep. I can't keep searching for answers. Do I even really want to see what happened? Of course not, but I have to know. Idiot! No wonder you're losing your mind. . .

> *The broken pieces and black of night can't stand in the light of God.*

One part of your brain is irrational, instinctual, terrified, and screaming at you to hide and run away from life because you and your loved ones are in danger. The other side of your brain, the quieter, rational side, tries desperately to break into the conversation and help you stay in the fight and not give up.

It's okay, breathe. They're not real. None of this is real. You are safe. You're not there. This is not happening right now. Get out of this room and go do something. Go to the gym. Go to the mall. Just get out of your room. Do you know where you are? It's okay, just breathe, this isn't real. They're not real. None of this is real.

While you fiercely try to win the battle for your mind, society expects you to continue functioning and participating in life as if you are normal. So, despite the gnawing demons at the edge of your mind wooing you deeper and deeper into the black hole of despair and destruction, somehow you still have to figure out how to work, eat, go to school, and be part of a family. Bonus points if you can do that without letting on that you are slowly losing contact with reality and falling further into the abyss.

This is what psychological distress after a trauma feels like, when your entire being turns on you and you can no longer tell up from down. According to Dr. Bessel van der Kolk, a pioneer in trauma and the body, when a person experiences trauma, the part of the brain that controls cognitive and executive functioning such as rational thought, memory, and interpretation of events, shuts down and goes quiet. This ability of the cognitive brain to go offline during trauma allows the limbic system—the instinctual center of your brain—to take over. Our minds were designed to sense danger and give us the best opportunity to get away from that danger alive.

After the danger has passed, the limbic system is designed to go quiet and allow the cognitive and executive functions to take over again to make sense of and recover from what a

During trauma, the rational brain goes offline leaving you with just your animal instincts.

person has just experienced. In most people, this system is virtually flawless, and they can recover from trauma fairly quickly and move forward in life. However, in some people the system gets stuck, and their instinctual brain continues overriding the rational brain, resulting in the symptoms associated with PTSD and other psychiatric disorders (see appendix A). One of my clients described it this way:

> *It's like you step outside of you. You're watching yourself run, panic, and want to disappear. On one hand, the part of you that is watching this happen realizes that there's nothing there, it's a noise, a scent, or sight that is completely harmless. You know that smelling stale beer is nothing more than gross. The other part of you is paralyzed with fear because the smell of stale beer means he's coming for me. I am watching, but I can't do anything about the panic, and when I finally work myself up and vomit, it's like then I am able to come back together and look at what just happened. It's been fifty years, and I still freeze, panic, and retreat inward when I smell it. If this happens when I'm out in public, it's really awkward trying to explain to people what's going on. I usually don't go out. I never go to happy hour with my coworkers. And my husband and I have to avoid normal places where people drink*

*alcohol because I just can't seem to stay together
and not react.*

Studies indicate that many of the symptoms associated with mental illnesses such as depression, anxiety, obsessive-compulsive disorder, and some personality disorders, are rooted in trauma. In my own clinical practice, this has been a constant in my clients. Very few people I encounter who are experiencing symptoms of mental illness do not have a history of trauma. This emerging concept demands that practitioners and caregivers begin to view mental illness from the perspective of trauma to effectively help those who are suffering.

When working or living with a person who has symptoms of a mental illness, especially when those symptoms are confusing, hurtful, frustrating, chaotic, and not following the description of how a person *should* appear who has these illnesses, it is important to ask yourself why. This is where all the so-called professionals failed me when I asked for help. They never bothered to look deeper. Clinicians are trained to use the *Diagnostic and Statistical Manual* to render diagnoses and understand how a person is suffering, but most people who encounter these individuals are not specifically trained to look for and address the role of trauma in what their client is experiencing.

People who have been traumatized rarely present their symptoms in a nice, neat, understandable package.

When victims lose the executive functioning part of their brain, the areas that control sensation, perception, boundaries, and a social filter are also gravely impaired. Therefore, people who have suffered trauma can behave and think in ways that are of great concern to themselves and other people. They can experience hallucinations, delusions, dissociation, paranoia, hypervigilance, and occasionally exert violence towards themselves or others. In rare instances, people may act out the memories that are haunting them while they sleep, which can be devastating.

Additionally, individuals can get stuck in the memories, or experience flashbacks and lose touch with reality, causing them to go missing or completely change their identities. While these reactions are rare, they are common enough that it warrants attention. That's why it is important to truly understand a person's history of trauma when they seek help or suddenly become someone you do not know. Every person I have met who suffers in this way, including myself, feels shame, self-hatred, hopelessness, and are devastated by the things that they do and say which they cannot control. They feel betrayed by their bodies and minds and express what is happening inside of them.

People suffering from trauma believe there's no safe place to escape or get help. So they pretend they're okay. And each day they wake up and try to believe that they're going to get better on their own. They want to believe they are fine, but they continue falling deeper into the pit where they can feel their breath being taken from them. The pit where the more they struggle to regain their footing, the farther down into the slime they sink.

Education and training in this area among mental health professionals is woefully lacking. This creates a dichotomy wherein you know that things are not as they should be, that something is wrong, and when you seek help you realize not many people are able to effectively treat the mind and body responses to trauma.

Trauma doesn't go away if you try hard enough, if you pray hard enough, if you eat right and exercise, or if you do enough good in the world. Many well-meaning people stick by someone immediately after they have survived a traumatic event that ravages their lives, but most grow tired and give up when the person doesn't seek help or recover fast enough. PTSD will not simply get better over time. PTSD causes measurable changes in the body, brain, mind, and spirit, and without professional help it will continue to disrupt and destroy the victim, despite all their best effort or intentions.

When a person experiences trauma, regardless of the type of trauma or the age in which the trauma is experienced, the brain has an extremely well-developed protective mechanism that allows them to survive the traumatic experience. However, the age of a person, or experiencing continuous or repeated exposure to traumatic events, does affect how that person continues to respond in the midst of it and afterward. Children, for example, do not have the cognitive or emotional maturity to understand what happened to them. They do not have the words to articulate their experience. Oftentimes, many adults cannot even articulate what they survived and how they're responding. When a person cannot comprehend nor express or discuss it—and they do not have a healthy support network on which to fall back and feel safe—their minds cannot heal.

This results in prolonged reactions to trauma, like we see in people suffering from treatment-resistant and chronic PTSD. The mechanisms in the brain that allow people to process information and make sense out of the events they experience are effectively turned off. Unless a person who is suffering from this immensely debilitating, devastating, and shame-filled experience is provided with a safe place to heal and to begin accessing those critical cognitive functions, they will stay in the cycle of trauma— or find another way to stop the pain. Safety and support is a crucial factor in predicting whether or not a person will develop prolonged trauma reactions.

PTSD will not just get better, it will not heal with the passage of time.

For a traumatized person to heal, they must believe that their environment is safe and that they are not in immediate, fatal danger. Too often, however, the opposite is the case—their stories are dismissed and their pain minimized. If they do not act the way they are expected to act and respond, if they do not immediately begin to express distressed behavior, then they can be overlooked and ignored. When this happens, the person experiences the additional trauma of being dismissed. They begin to question why they can't get over it or why "no one can figure out what is wrong." They are unable to find safety and will continue down the spiral into the deeper depths of their own personal hell until they and others do not recognize them anymore.

This loss of identity devastates their relationships, careers, and their hope for healing. Trauma wreaks havoc on every system of your being, without your explicit consent. Believing that you are just a victim, owning that identity perpetuates the trauma and suffering, and builds resistance against treatment. Although unintentional, it is always counterproductive and eventually destructive for that person.

The mind may be the first part of their being that suffers trauma, it will not be the only casualty of this war. Oftentimes, the physical manifestation of chronic, untreated trauma, can be more obvious than the carefully hidden and masked psychological distress.

5

THIS IS YOUR BODY
ON TRAUMA

*When you shut down emotion, you're also affecting your
immune system, your nervous system. So the repression of
emotion, which is a survival strategy, then becomes a source
of physiological illness later on*

—Gabor Maté

"**I** can't explain why I'm in so much pain. My entire
body hurts. It's like I've been hit repeatedly by a
train. I can barely get out of bed, my skin hurts to touch,
my joints are barely moving. I can barely put a thought
together, and I feel like I am just not doing well."

"Well, there is no medical reason that I can see for
what you're describing. We know that you have emotional
problems. Maybe you need to see a psychiatrist and get
some medications. If you start accepting that the pain

isn't real, you'll stop coming in here complaining about pain that doesn't really exist. Maybe if you lost weight and started doing something other than laying around, you'd feel better."

Wow, I can't believe she actually said that. What does she know? I know this is real, I'm not just imagining these symptoms. Why did I bother coming here and asking for help? I know better. I'll figure this out and then tell her what is wrong and force her to get me the help I need.

I woke up one day, soon after living through the shootings at Columbine and realized that I was in excruciating pain. My body hurt in ways that it never had before, and I could barely get out of bed to find the bottle of ibuprofen. I had been overweight growing up and had continued that pattern after the shootings, so I was used to being uncomfortable. But this was different. Instinctively I knew that this pain was not due to my lack of exercise or fast-food diet and alcohol consumption. I knew that much, but I did not know anything else.

I also had this inexplicable pain in my right elbow and upper arm that was new. *I remember this pain when I was running out the door. Maybe I hit it on the door frame? But that should have healed by now, right?* This was my introduction to the concept of "body memories." Like the idea of phantom limb pain, body memories are the physical reminders of injuries that occurred during trauma that have already healed. For me, every year in April, to this day, I suddenly have this pain in my arm. It's not nearly as bad now. I know what it is, and it's usually a brief flash, a short-lived pain that subsides after the anniversary passes.

My involvement in athletics pretty much ended the day of the shootings. I began to wonder if the problem was a challenging job, lack of sleep, and the horrible habits of a college student—or if it was something else.

After the "professionals" determined they couldn't diagnose a "normal" reason for my symptoms, I decided to deal with the pain myself. However, my inability to function on a "normal" level alarmed me, so I reluctantly went to my family doctor when I came home for a school break. Not surprisingly, the response involved a combination of "well we know you have emotional issues," and "the only thing you can do is exercise and diet."

In addition to the debilitating pain, I experienced levels of incomprehensible exhaustion and inability to clear my thoughts. I felt like I was physically off. I couldn't exercise enough, eat enough healthy food, really do anything enough to feel like my old self again. My body felt like it was barely hanging on by a thread, as if I was going to collapse any moment. This began an almost ten-year struggle for answers, diagnoses, and effective treatment that ended when I discovered what I thought would be the answer.

Fibromyalgia. A syndrome that no one knew anything about . . . again. *Great. What does this even mean? There really is nothing about me that will be understood, accepted, or easily fixed.*

Once I received the correct diagnosis, I immediately balked at the treatment they assigned me. I couldn't understand why I should take an antidepressant when I didn't feel depressed. And I didn't want to begin taking narcotics and end up addicted to pain medicine, so I chose not to participate in their treatments. This created more problems, because again the doctor decided that if I was not going to do what they wanted me to, the pain and inability to function *must* be in my head, and now I was a "problem patient."

In addition to my constant immeasurable pain, I began to lose hope because chronic pain is miserable to endure. However, by this time, I had already self-diagnosed my PTSD and began seeking effective treatment on my own that didn't involve antipsychotic medication that created even more of a zombie than I was already. I decided again to seek out alternative treatments to what the professionals described because I knew they were wrong about my suffering. If I couldn't trust the "professionals" to take care of me, I would take matters into my own hands and take care of myself.

Only two years ago, I acquiesced and began taking traditional medications to relieve the symptoms. A fibromyalgia specialist who understood my concerns, *explained* why the medications helped the pain. The most difficult aspect of this journey, however, was not the long delay in finding relief from my symptoms but realizing my relief from pain did not mean I was now physiologically sound. I continued to struggle with an inexplicable variety of physical symptoms that were not directly connected to each other. I was the consummate enigma for the medical profession, a constellation of symptoms without any identifiable cause or treatment, and no one seemed in a hurry to understand.

When a person experiences trauma, if they are injured during the attack, those physical injuries tend to eventually heal in one way or another. Only recently, pioneers in PTSD treatment report that the response in your brain to experiencing trauma creates physical changes in the body as well. When someone finally decided to try and understand trauma and how the mind and body responds to these events, the evidence indicated that physiological pain and other distressing physiological symptoms are the body's way of reconciling the traumatic event that remains an unhealed, festering wound.

According to Peter Levine, an early PTSD researcher and proponent of mind-body treatment, during a traumatic event, our limbic system sends a cascade of hormones and chemicals that flood into our body to help us survive. I discussed this briefly in chapter four. This fight-or-flight system, is an automatic response. When this system is functioning correctly, the body is flooded with hormones that allows our rapid response to the event and the onslaught subsides once the threat has been removed. It is a perfectly designed system that gets stuck when an individual is not able to receive the proper support and treatment after experiencing trauma.

However, when a person does not have a support network, internal coping strategies, or the opportunity

Trauma causes physical changes and symptoms in your body as well.

to receive adequate and effective trauma-focused treatment, their limbic system never resets. The fight-or-flight mode stays in the on position long after the threat has been neutralized.

The limbic system comprises part of what is known as the reptilian or animal brain, the area of our brain that responds to a fatal threat. When activated, it causes our heart to pump faster, our breathing to pick up speed, our adrenaline to rush, and our hormones and neurotransmitters to flood our brain and body with life-saving measures. This explains why our hearts race, we breathe rapidly, our eyes dilate, digestion stops, and our body shakes with tremors when we experience traumatic events.

The one thing that this part of the brain does not do, is think.

The limbic system shares no responsibility with thought, reason, rationality, or any type of cognitive function. Its only purpose is to react to the threat and stay alive. In those moments of terror, we really don't need to think about what we are doing or understand why, we just need to do it. When this system gets stuck, when it repeats a continual loop of thoughts and perceptions that everything you experience is a life-threatening event, the impact on the rest of the brain and body is monumental.

The field of neuropsychology has shed a great deal of light on the brain-body system, especially when exposed to trauma. Every other aspect of life requires cognitive functioning. We must be able to think, to interpret what we are seeing, hearing, smelling, tasting, and touching. We should be able to filter out inconsequential information to stay focused on the task at hand and achieve what we have set out to accomplish. If we are constantly distracted by peripheral noises, like doors slamming shut or people talking around us, we will not be able to finish any task, let alone one that we truly want to complete.

For people stuck in the loop of a broken limbic system, this is exactly what happens. When that system is on at all times, there is no room for cognitive functioning. We may be able to endure a minor problem, but our ability to perceive, interpret, understand, and think rationally is critically impaired. Therefore, sufferers may struggle holding a job, their performance ratings dip, they cannot seem to handle simple cognitive tasks (let alone multitask), and they find it difficult tracking and remembering conversations or knowing what they need to be doing. They often struggle in school and will likely notice a reduction in their ability to maintain previous performance levels in academia.

People suffering from unhealed trauma are not purposely making mistakes, getting off task, or struggling to accomplish everyday responsibilities that used to be easy or should be easy. They struggle because their brain is out of control, their limbic system is continually sending the message that they need to react, and they cannot simply turn it off and "get over it." Unhealed trauma creates new neural pathways in the brain that change the way we process information so that everything runs through the fight-or-flight system instead of the systems that allow for meaning and interpretation of input. To turn the cognitive functioning part of the brain back on and change this dysfunction, you must reset the limbic system so that it no longer overrides the rational, cognitive brain.

We also understand that unhealed trauma significantly impacts a person's ability to retain information and form memories. The brain's hippocampus plays a significant role in the development, classification, and retention of memories. Normally, the hippocampus functions in conjunction with the other parts of the brain that provide meaning, context, and interpretation of events to effectively code memories into their proper locations.

However, in the traumatized brain, the hippocampus has no context with which to understand and interpret the traumatic event. This creates a cataclysmic failure in the memory system, resulting in the trauma survivor's experience of intrusive thoughts, flashbacks, and occasionally psychotic symptoms such as hallucinations.

The brain is desperately trying to understand what happened so that the traumatic information can be encoded into the proper memory location and the brain can move on to other, more important tasks, but is unable to do so because of the trauma. This causes the brain to "remind" the survivor of what happened in hopes that the other parts of the brain can offer context and interpretation to create the memory.

When the fight-or-flight system stays stuck in the on position for a long time, the body eventually responds to the ongoing overproduction of hormones such as cortisol and begins to develop physical symptoms that are rooted in the trauma. Research shows that many people who survive trauma experience debilitating pain, stomach and digestive issues, heart and lung issues, as well as an increased risk in the development of certain cancers. Our bodies were not designed to be continually flooded with these hormones, in a constant state of stress. When our systems malfunction, the stored energy, emotions, and chemicals must be resolved. They don't just dissipate.

The world is broken and full of tragic events: natural disasters, wars, rapes, murders, domestic violence, and mass shootings. When something traumatic happens to you, it leads to a perfect storm where the body and mind both begin to break down in response. The physical symptoms of unhealed and chronic trauma often drive people to the doctor for help. They don't realize or believe that the severe stomach troubles, pain, heart palpitations, confusion, or memory loss are all physiological symptoms of unhealed trauma(s).

Our culture has conditioned us to believe that the medical profession can heal anything. So when the doctors return with a non-diagnosis and cannot offer a physical reason for our pain, it further pushes us into the hole of silent and intense suffering. We begin to convince ourselves that if there really was a problem, a doctor could figure it out, so that must mean that we really are "crazy." Other than the severe hopelessness these beliefs can induce, if we truly believe no hope exists for relieving our physical pain, then there must be no hope for healing our emotional pain. The truth is, there absolutely *is* hope for healing from both physical and emotional pain, just not necessarily in the traditional, Western medicine belief system.

I will always just be that person who will forever be in pain. Nothing is actually wrong, no one can figure it out, so I guess I'm stuck with it. How am I going to survive with all of this stuff? When do I get my relief or at least a break?

I believed I could never truly be free to live the life I wanted to live, even if I did heal from the PTSD. I convinced myself that physical healing was for other people and that I surely didn't meet the qualifications for someone who could be healed. That is, until I began to understand the intricate design of our unified being. God didn't create us as a separate body, separate brain, separate soul. He created us so they would function together, as one.

That means what affects one part will also, undeniably, affect the rest.

When I was first introduced to a form of mind-body healing named Splankna, I immediately began to see the effectiveness of this treatment. Already, I had explored alternative healing methods such as massage, acupuncture, homeopathy, and anything that incorporated mind-body healing, but I had not been exposed to such an intensely studied and crafted method that also included my own Christian belief system.

I was intrigued, to say the least. This was an answer to prayer, the missing link in the full and complete healing from traumatic pasts, so I eagerly immersed myself in the protocol, both as a client and a practitioner. Because this treatment protocol addressed the mind-body-soul connection, I experienced true and complete healing. After a few sessions specifically addressing some issues in my long journey, I was completely free of the fibromyalgia pain that I had endured for eighteen years.

I now know firsthand that hope for healing from both the physical and psychological pain of trauma is possible. As I now understand the intimate connection between the mind and body, I no longer shy away from acknowledging that the pain, at least partially, is in my head. The intimate and powerful connections between our minds and our bodies cannot be ignored. Too much is at stake for those of us who want to find healing.

6

SO THIS IS LOVE?

We repeat what we don't repair.
—Christine Langley-Obaugh

This guy is amazing! I mean, Okay, he's not exactly what I would have wanted, but I can't really afford to be picky. It seems like he likes me, and he's okay, so I guess this is it. I mean, really, who else is going to want to be with me?

In my mind, as a result of the horrific bullying and cruelty from the boys in whom I'd been previously interested, I was a horrific human being: fat, ugly, and completely shattered into millions of pieces. The fact that he even paid attention to me meant that it "was meant to be." He liked me, but he didn't think like me, believe in God the way I did, respect me, or even treat me the way I desired to be treated, but he "wanted me."

In the five years after surviving the Columbine High School shooting, I engaged in many self-destructive behaviors, but none with permanent and inescapable consequences like what would have happened had I stayed with him. I just did not see it until it was almost too late.

This is another example of God's extreme grace, mercy, and unflinching forgiveness for me and for anyone who seeks Him. He protected me from myself and this damaged and destructive relationship even though I didn't ask Him to. He took care of me when I didn't want to take care of myself. Eventually I broke free.

I did not immediately realize, however, that my acceptance of an emotionally unavailable and emotionally abusive relationship was symptomatic of how my trauma tainted my life and thoughts. This diseased and putrid way in which I viewed myself and my value in relationships began long before the Columbine shootings, long before I had conscious memory of embracing this distorted way of thinking.

For as long as I could remember, I felt unworthy, so embracing a relationship where I had little value or worth beyond what I could "give" was not a totally foreign concept. It just took on a life of its own after the shootings and threatened to engulf in unquenchable flames what little bit of fight for survival remained.

Trauma destroyed my ability to like myself, believe in myself, and fight for myself in every way, but it became most destructive in my relationships.

I am a walking advertisement for damaged goods, and rather than fight against that image, I embraced it and allowed it to corrupt my thinking and behavior. This poison infiltrated every relationship in such a way that I could no longer see it. I searched for relationships that validated what I already believed about myself, but then I took them a step further to see how destructive and miserable I could make them. I would push my partner by not attempting to control my emotional lability and rages to see if they really wanted me. I had the mentality that I would lay all of my brokenness and ugliness out there and see what happened. Needless to say, exposing every demon you fight on a first date was not the healthiest way to probe someone's interest.

When God created us, His design did not include self-loathing, self-hatred, disgust, or shame; that is the mark of the enemy of our soul. But I festered in those thoughts for so long that I didn't realize what I was doing. I just let the riptide pull me even farther into destruction. At this point, my experience of complex trauma, multiple traumatic events forced to exist one on top of the other, became clear. My complex trauma almost killed me, and had it not killed me, it would have surely resulted in the permanent destruction of who God created me to be.

Trauma destroyed my ability to love and believe in myself.

Most of my conversations with well-meaning friends and family went something like this:

"How can you continue to live like this? Don't you see what's really happening?"

"What else am I supposed to do? I don't want to be alone, and he's the only guy who's ever looked at me."

"You are better than this, and you deserve better than him!"

"Oh yeah? Well let me know when you see the good guys lining up to be with me."

You see, I am a relationship-oriented person. I deeply and desperately desire intimacy in all my relationships, especially if I am going to be vulnerable and share the darkness of my past. God created all of us to long for relationships that are deep, vulnerable, respectful, and full of unconditional love and true intimacy.

For a short time in my life, I fully embraced relationships in the way that God created them to exist for me. I still am unsure when that started to morph into what it had become. Slowly and stealthily, the fog of disillusion, disgust, self-hatred, and shame crept into my mind. This imperceptible, internal agitation of rapidly devolving self-hatred filled the crevices of my mind, eventually overtaking my cognitive functioning and hijacking the person I was created to be and devastating almost every relationship I entered. Something inside my brain clicked off when I was in a relationship.

What are you doing? This is not how this is supposed to be. You would never do this if you were not with this guy! What is wrong with you? Do you even know who you are anymore?

Intimacy, a craving God places in every person was undeniably missing and broken in my life. True intimacy requires a relationship with other people. We cannot achieve intimacy the way our soul craves without another person, but very few people know what this means or can understand what it looks like.

As a society, we spend way too much time looking to Hollywood and binge-watching our favorite television shows, to define intimacy and healthy relationships. We willingly dissociate from the reality of what we truly desire and immerse ourselves in the lies and manipulation of the media and what other people tell us we should be experiencing in our relationships . . . without the added complication of trauma.

Trauma complicates this desperate need for intimacy and relationship even further. The first lesson we learn after we experience trauma is that the world is no longer a safe place, people are no longer safe. This is magnified exponentially when your trauma is perpetrated by people who were supposed to love you, respect you, and provide safety and security in your life. When someone close to you destroys the fabric of your self-identity and shoves your ideas regarding that relationship into a place that cannot be reached, the result is a complete disruption of not just that relationship, but every future relationship.

The foundation of all relationships begins with trust. We must be able to trust the person with whom we develop a relationship to feel safe enough to be vulnerable. To be ourselves. A relationship that lacks complete trust in the other person will perpetually struggle and likely fall apart because neither person is willing or able to be completely open and honest with the other.

The basis of trust is built on your interactions with the other person: what is said, what is done, if confidences are kept, and most importantly, how the other person responds when you expose your dark side.

So often we present a social media–worthy appearance where everything is perfect in hopes that others will not see the parts we want to hide. This is impossible with intimate relationships. No matter how hard we try to present the best sides of us, life will always intervene and reveal those parts we hate, that make us feel ashamed. We tell ourselves things like:

> "He never used to be like this. If he had been like this before we were married, I never would have married him!"

> "If she only knew what I did while I was over there, she'd be horrified. She'd leave me and take the kids. There's no way I can ever tell her what I went through. Some things have to be hidden."

> "I don't know what I did wrong. I don't think I can keep going like this. Something is missing here. I don't know if we ever had it."

"I can't tell him. I just want him to love me. To be nice, to spend time with me, to make me a priority in our relationship. I don't know how that is wrong. Aren't we supposed to do that? He'd never love me if he knew."

"He's the best I'll ever get. I mean, look at me! He's really doing me a favor being with me. Yeah, he pushes me around, and most of the time I'm scared of what he'll do, but where else am I going to go?"

Oftentimes, this fear of exposure keeps traumatized individuals from engaging in healthy and truly meaningful relationships. Either their pain is still hidden, and no one knows what they've suffered, or they experience so much shame or brokenness because of their trauma, they fear pushing the other person away with their pain. No matter the reason behind the self-imposed isolation or destructive relationship, the result is the same: the traumatized person believes they have been able to keep themselves safe in a situation that evokes feelings of fear.

If we do not feel like we can safely trust the other person with the deepest pain of our past, we will self-regulate that relationship so that the other person never gets close enough to see that side of us.

Traumatized individuals also tend to find themselves attracted to destructive or abusive relationships. Trauma causes an intensely devastating separation between who we thought we were and who we now must be. We struggle understanding our new label of *survivor* or *victim* and must figure out how to reconcile who we were before the trauma and who we became as a result of the trauma. Without a doubt, the person before and after our immersion in hell is markedly different.

People who do not receive support and treatment for their trauma tend to turn this mistaken identity inward and begin a pattern of self-destructive behaviors that manifest in unhealthy and destructive relationships.

People who have suffered appalling physical or sexual abuse may find themselves flocking to perpetrators who will continue to hurt them in similar ways because it's the only thing that is familiar. A client relayed this struggle:

"Why do you think you need to suffer? Why do you keep hurting yourself?"

"I don't know. I think I deserve it. Everything was my fault anyway. I could have said no. I could have fought back. I didn't, so I deserve this."

"How could you have fought him off? You were a child; he was the adult. He was responsible for doing the right thing. You did nothing wrong."

"Well, Okay, maybe that's right, but what about all the other guys? I just kept going back for more. I just can't escape men who want to hurt me, so the problem must be me."

People who have suffered trauma in combat, in natural disasters, and unspeakable violence at the hands of strangers oftentimes develop such a negative view of themselves and others that they are attracted to others who will feed that negative view and push away relationships that will balance those thoughts and behaviors with truth and positivity.

The saddest and most defeating part of this relationship pattern is that traumatized individuals do not *want* to be in abusive relationships; they know on a visceral level that this is not who they want to be. They feel powerless to change their relationships in any meaningful way and feel as if it's not worth it to try because nothing will ever change. People who are traumatized feel stuck in their circumstances and struggle pulling themselves out of destructive relationships without help. Even in these relationships, the traumatized person knows they are not alone, that they have someone who they can interact with who is important to them in some way.

The fear of being alone, the fear of rejection, the fear of being too "messed up" for anyone to love, prevents traumatized people from being able to engage in healthy and intimate relationships, even when they desperately desire that connection.

That connection, however, leads to healing and restoration of safety in that person's life. The dichotomy of vulnerability leading to safety in the right relationships is difficult to believe for those who have suffered. This need for meaningful connection is often the missing piece in a relationship that sets the stage for all the other conflicts and difficulties that relationships endure. One of my clients related this struggle to me:

"Why did you both decide to come and see me? How can I help you?"

"I feel like we're strangers. We don't talk about anything that matters. He has no idea who I am, what matters to me, what drives me. I feel like he doesn't want to have anything to do with me anymore."

"That definitely makes everything more challenging. What about you? What do you want to work on in here?"

"I don't know. I guess she may be right, but I have nothing to say. Every time she wants to talk about something she thinks is important, I just shut down. I don't see why we have to work on anything, I mean, it's fine."

"Is what she's saying accurate? Do you know her, want to know her?"

"Of course, I do. I just don't think that we need to talk about it all the time. Besides, there are things about me she doesn't know, and I'm good with that."

"What do you mean, there are things I don't know about you? What are you hiding? What don't you want me to see?"

"This is what I'm talking about, why I don't care anymore. Why does she have to know everything about me? It's not like she'd understand anyway. She'd just end up leaving me. I don't want that. I want her to be here; I just don't want her to know."

Your partner's inability or choice not to try and understand what happens when you have an episode, shut down, or lash out, leads to the assumption that they *obviously know that you are too broken to ever be who you were before.* Continuing to hide the darkness, the fears, the shame, the lies that you tell yourself about the trauma, yourself, and others seems like the safest option. However, this pattern of secrecy perpetuates the belief that you are unlovable because of what happened to you and what you experienced.

To truly be free in relationships, to develop the intimacy and companionship that your soul, mind, and body crave, you must begin to let down the fortified walls around your mind, body, and soul, and invite worthy people into your suffering. The people who are worth your effort, those who don't run away in the difficult moments, and who do not blame you for your reaction to the trauma are the ones you allow to stay with you through the healing process.

Unless they have experienced trauma, they may have a hard time understanding what is going on. In a worthy relationship, one that is worth fighting for, they will want to keep trying. Those are the people that you fight to let inside, for whom you fight the urge to run and hide when your demons come knocking in the middle of the night to tell you lies. Worthy people are the ones who will help you find yourself again, who will bathe your wounds and help you put the pieces of your broken heart back together again . . . if you will let them.

So much of how we experience relationships and life after trauma leads us to believe the lie that the only way we can control and tame the demons is by keeping all our pain and suffering inside and never letting anyone see what we are fighting against. Not only can this lead to suicidal thoughts and behaviors to escape the torment, but it almost always leads to the destruction of the relationships we value the most.

Instinctively, we know that we are safe with that person, but we struggle to let them see the depth of our pain and suffering because we believe the lie that *if they knew who I really was what I really did, what I really think, then they could never love me.*

This lie can become an identifying part of our relationships because we truly believe this about ourselves. We accept and own the lie that tells us, because this happened to us, what we had to do to survive, what we struggle with every single day, we are and always will be, unlovable.

Relationships with traumatized people add a level of difficulty absent in other relationships. Traumatized people tend to traverse back and forth between feeling safe enough to be vulnerable and feeling the urge to retreat inside of themselves. However, that doesn't necessarily mean that relationships will always be bad or that in the midst of your hardest moments with the people you love that you have "gone too far this time," or that "there's no way to come back" from what has happened.

We are all primed to crave love, intimacy, and relationship, it's only over when you decide that it's not worth fighting for.

God created us for relationships but not bad or superficial ones. Ultimately, healthy relationships with other people should point to a real and intimate relationship with our Creator. God desires a relationship with us and even provides redemption and healing in relationships. He longs to reach into your broken heart, broken relationships, and broken self-relationship, and place his soothing, healing balm on all the red-hot fractures.

> *We are all created to crave love, intimacy, and relationships.*

God knows the depth of your pain when no one else does. When all your other relationships seem broken beyond repair and you feel hopeless that you will ever emerge from the pain, He is right next to you, waiting for you to fall into Him and stop trying to fix it alone.

He sees you when you're at your weakest and worst, and He still longs to wrap you in His arms and soothe your breathtaking anguish and restore your hope in others, in yourself and in your relationships.

Maybe you are thinking, "I can't believe this is my life. I waited, I did what I was supposed to do, why is my marriage like this? I don't want to feel pain like this anymore. I don't know what to do." Lean into God in the pain. This means crying, screaming, cussing, being raw and broken before Him, asking for something to change. It doesn't mean censoring yourself as if you could somehow hide the truth of the pain in your soul from the One who created you.

Lean into God in the pain. Don't hide the pain in your soul from the One who created you.

Even if the relationship never changes, when you let Him comfort you, lead you, soothe the raw wounds that threaten to overtake you, even then, He will change you. He will give you peace during pain, and He will show you how to escape an abusive or destructive relationship (see appendix C).

This is how you work through the hurt of a broken and seemingly hopeless relationship. You cannot fix it on your own, especially when you are trying to keep your head above the water so you don't drown in your own suffering. You reach out; you seek help; you take care of your own mental, physical, and spiritual health. If something changes in your relationships, great. If not, *you* will be healthy no matter what. That is true freedom in relationships. Heal yourself, and oftentimes, the brokenness that seems impossible to heal starts to change as well.

7

THE BATTLE BEGINS

It's hard to beat a person who never gives up.

—Babe Ruth

About five years after the Columbine High School shootings, my life was completely out of control, in mental chaos, and literally in a place I never should have been. I was engaging in behaviors with men that were destructive and harmful, and I was careless with how I spoke to and about other people. My level of rage, and at times intentionally careless behaviors, led to many situations that could have caused significant damage to myself and other people. In one instant, during a confrontation where I was "thrown to the wolves" despite my counselor being present, I made a comment about how everyone would be happier if I accidentally drove off the side of the mountain. This was misinterpreted, and I was put in the back of a police car in handcuffs and taken to a hospital for evaluation. It took the doctor approximately five minutes to understand what really happened, but the entire situation caused significant but completely unnecessary re-traumatization.

I had completely lost any recognition of who I was and was barely existing. During this black hole, when I was flailing about desperately trying to find something or someone to keep me from drowning, I found the ability to reach out and grab hold of God and found that He had already been holding my head above the water.

Jesus, I can't do this anymore! What is wrong with me? What is wrong with You? Aren't you supposed to help me, to intervene, to fix this? I cried out.

How can I help you? God replied. *You won't let me in, you keep trying to do everything your way. You've never stepped back, let Me take control, and let Me hold onto you while I work*

Ouch, that's fun. Of course that's right. I've been trying to control everything for so long, I'm terrified of what my life would be like if I give control to You. But maybe it's time to do something different. I'm going to die if I don't. Okay, God. Your turn.

I began to understand that I was either going to die, destroy anything that I wanted from this life, or end up institutionalized somewhere participating in the pharmaceutical zombie apocalypse.

I was frozen in the fear of who I had become. I was no longer sure what I was capable of, because I had done so many things that I never would have thought I would have been capable of. Self-hatred permeated my thinking; I felt weak and pathetic, and I knew that if I did not get myself together, I would never accomplish any of the hopes and dreams from long ago.

I needed to decide where I wanted to go and who I wanted to be.

I can't just keep waking up and waiting to see what happens. I need to start trying to participate in life again.

Facing the crossroads of my life, I knew my entire existence was at stake. A choice needed to be made in that moment. I could continue taking the path I was on, knowing where that path was going to lead, or I could somehow find the courage and strength to choose the road that was beginning to materialize in front of me.

In one of these moments of clarity, I buried my face in my hands and cried out to God in a way that I didn't even know was humanly possible. I wept bitterly and called out to God, fully expressing the depravity, the depth of pain, grief, loss, resentment, and horror that was revolving around in my mind and in my soul. For the first time in my life, I saw a glimmer of light.

This catharsis cleared my head enough and gave me the strength to get up one more time and make the calls to get the help I needed. Surrendering to Him gave me faith to believe that *this time* it was going to work, something was going to change.

I would love to tell you that what followed was a rapid and almost instantaneous healing and rebirth of my identity and new existence, but that would be laying a trail of false hope.

Why is this so hard? Shouldn't this have gotten easier by this point? I'm doing everything I think I'm supposed to, why am I still struggling? Shouldn't I be back to normal by now?

Most of the work on my path to healing occurred in the next few years. As time continued to pass, however, I began to understand that when you have complex trauma and PTSD, each time you find success in one area, you peel back another layer of chaos and pain that you didn't even know existed.

The painful and indescribably horrific events of my past left my limbic system switch in the on position and me constantly feeling afraid of everything. I cannot think back and identify something or some situation that did not evoke a sense of terror when I was experiencing it.

I cannot remember a time in my life when I felt completely safe and able to be myself and not be on guard all the time. To *begin* to heal, I needed to create my own safe space. I needed to actively and intentionally remind myself that I am safe, and either escape to my physical safe place or use imagery and mindfulness to imagine being there until my limbic system was calm enough to hear truth.

I guess this could work, I told myself. *I've always wanted a cabin in the woods with a huge library, a roaring fire, and a huge balcony open to see the wildlife. I think I will use that as my mental safe place.*

Even still, when I am in a negative space I forget to use the tools that have helped me in the past. As much as I want a quick fix, a magic pill to undo what was done, I must remember that healing from severe and complex trauma and PTSD is ongoing, even when the symptoms have all but disappeared.

This person that I am today, the woman that has fought, clawed, bled, and screamed her way into existence, is someone who, for the most part, I like. I realize now that the people and events meant for my annihilation, physically and psychologically, failed at destroying me. They took a large part of my life, they shattered my childhood and devastated my identity, but they did not and will not ever succeed in destroying me.

One of the most important lessons I learned was that I could choose to let my past define who I am, or I can be who I was created to be and thrive in my life, *despite* my past. I finally realized that:

"I can't keep letting them win. I feel like every time I struggle, it's them taking ground in my life. I refuse to let my past destroy my future anymore."

"Now you're fighting. You can give your past ownership of your future, you can allow the enemy to control and manipulate who you were meant to be, or you can choose to reclaim what was taken."

"I just wish I didn't have to do that in the first place! It seems so unfair that I have to fight like this just to be free. I didn't like who I was before, but it seemed easier to deal with than this!"

You can choose to let your past define you or live your life despite your past.

This is the most difficult part in the healing journey. Trauma shatters your identity and sense of reality. A part of you desperately wants to return to the way things were, and you're angry that you're forced to deal with the pain. Your trauma feels terribly unfair, and you wish you could pretend it never happened. While this sounds good, you also know that no matter how much you bargain and beg for some other reality, this is now part of who you are.

Refusing to accept what happened to you dishonors the pain and empowers it to destroy you. By this I mean that when you pretend that you are "fine," that "nothing happened" or that it was "no big deal and you're over it," despite the fact that you're dying a thousand deaths deep inside your soul, you are further distancing yourself from who you really are, staying disconnected from your true identity.

None of us who have experienced this kind of pain enjoy the chaos and suffering that results from those moments; however, we must accept that the pain, suffering, and hurt we experience is part of who we are. Dismissing that pain, minimizing the trauma and the negative impact it has taken on our lives and our identity, allows the hurt and the chaos to continue.

It gives permission to the people who have hurt us to continue hurting us long after they are gone.

We know, on a subconscious level that we are barely breathing, and every time we dismiss the struggle, we sink deeper and deeper into the quicksand that threatens to bury us alive.

The healing that resulted after I made the choice to accept that I was going to need to redefine who I was meant to be and who I wanted to be, regardless of where I had been and what I experienced, was profound. For me, every small step forward was followed by a cataclysmic avalanche that pushed me back farther than where I had begun. My propensity to be blind to what is really going on in me, to fail to accept or see the good things in favor of highlighting the negative, threatened to keep me from ever climbing out of the deep valley that I had sunk into.

The sometimes-treacherous journey up the jagged side of your mountain doesn't often let you see that the peak is just above you and that you are almost free of the struggle. The fight to reclaim or redefine who you are will always be is incredibly hard. It is much easier to sit in the pain and suffering, even knowing that it will slowly kill you, because it is familiar and becomes what you think is a safe place.

It can still be difficult to see that I am a different, healthier person today than I was twenty years ago, or even ten years ago. Fortunately, I have people in my life whom I love and now can accept their words as truth, who help me believe that I have become a completely different person. I do not resemble the broken and self-destructive shell of a human I used to be, even on my bad days.

When you go through the fires of hell, when you feel like you've been forever chained in that place that you hate and you're trying to break free, you must first change your mind-set. This is where the ferocity of your battle for yourself takes place. Where you suffer the most casualties or gain the most ground.

Our thoughts control our emotions and our behaviors. If you cannot or will not change and control your thoughts, you will never break free from the behaviors and emotions that violate your sense of safety, your identity, and your life.

Fighting for your identity, for the life you *should* be living, instead of the life your traumas forced on you, starts in your mind. Willpower, physical strength, escape, or any other Band-Aid you try use to stop the continuous oozing from your trauma wounds that evokes change will never work. The choices you make every day to change the way you think about yourself, other people, and your trauma experience, determine whether you stand victorious at the end of the war or allow yourself to be another casualty.

8

THE WAR RAGES ON

Still. I rise.

—Maya Angelou

"**A**re you freaking kidding me? What is wrong with these people? It's 3:00 a.m., can't they do anything other than create chaos? I hate people."

The fire alarms were going off for what seemed like the hundredth time that week, and always in the middle of the night. Drunk and stoned freshman who decided to fully embrace their liberty from mom and dad thought it was hilarious to pull the fire alarm at 3:00 a.m. every single weekend night, terrorizing those of us who associated fire alarms with trauma and pain.

I mean, of course they aren't doing this on purpose. They don't know that there are Columbine survivors here and that their pranks are terrifying. But why do they have to do this? Can't they just be drunk and stupid somewhere else?

After only a few short weeks of enduring this nauseating flashback and nightmare-inducing prank, I began staying awake all night. I believed that if I could just stay awake in the darkness, the demons that were hunting me would not find me and I could rest when the sun came up.

After a couple days, I developed symptoms closely resembling psychosis. The longer this went on, the crazier I felt, and I finally decided to go to the school health center and talk to their doctor to see if I could maybe figure out how to sleep at night and not be terrorized.

"Doctor, I can't sleep. I'm a Columbine survivor and these idiot freshmen keep pulling the fire alarm and I wake up in a nightmare."

"How long has this been going on? What other symptoms do you have?"

"I haven't slept in about a week, at least no more than a couple hours during the day. I am edgy and feel like I'm freaking out all the time. I want to hide and plot all my escape routes from class . . . oh, and sometimes I see them coming through my dorm room wall to kill me."

After I explained my symptoms to him, emphasizing that I was a Columbine survivor as well, he looked at me and told me I must be having a psychotic schizophrenic break and put me on the strongest antipsychotic he thought would help.

Even though I knew he was wrong, I was so desperate for relief that I willingly, albeit naively, entered the pharmaceutical zombie apocalypse. I began shuffling through my days . . . but still couldn't find relief. The meds created horrible side effects (try explaining to your mom that you're lactating but not pregnant) and did absolutely nothing to fix my symptoms.

For the rest of my five years in oblivion after the shootings, I vacillated between a variety of different drugs—each worse than the next—and so-called treatments that seemed to do nothing except make my life more intolerable. Around that time I enrolled in some advanced psychology classes and realized that not only was I totally misdiagnosed (and dismissed) but completely overmedicated. I decided to force the correct diagnosis, and find the right kind of treatment that would help (see appendix B). I removed the incorrect and harmful labels ignorant doctors had placed on me and stopped taking the medications. This in and of itself was a fight, but I made the decision and refused to back down. I began treatment with an effective counselor, and together we worked on getting *me* back.

Until I found this counselor, I lacked an advocate who knew what was going on and would fight for me. My family was supportive, but they were at a loss because my brother responded quite differently to the shootings than me. Maybe, in part, because he was a freshman at the time and was able to return to the school and heal with his classmates. My fellow seniors never had this opportunity. They held many events during the year that followed, but those of us who left home to go to college and move forward were unintentionally left out.

I was broken and did not have anyone with the stamina or knowledge to put me back together again. So I had to fight. I fought every doctor so they would treat me the way that I needed to be treated and with a modicum of decency and respect. I fought to maintain my sanity and my world. I mostly did this poorly and with destructive behaviors, but I felt that if I just gave up, knowing the little bit of truth about what was going on, that I would completely fade into obscurity and would cease existing on any meaningful level to anyone.

I knew that I did not want to fade out of existence, and so I fought.

To this day, I am not completely sure where I found the strength to keep fighting. I felt I would never find the answer and that I was forever destined to be the broken vessel that I had become. The broken shell I was existing in was kept from fully forming around me because I continued to fight. Had I given up that fight, I would have faded into the dark unknown, undoubtedly never escaping from that place.

I knew enough to know that I wasn't experiencing a psychotic break and that the pharmacy I ingested daily did nothing but keep me chemically restrained. I knew that the professionals were either incredibly naive and ignorant in effective diagnosis and treatment, or they didn't care enough to ask the right questions. They treated me as if I was crazy, that it's impossible to *still* be suffering and to both have hallucinations of your trauma and *not* be psychotic.

No one wanted to listen, no one wanted to do the hard work required to effectively help me come back from the depths of hell.

From an early age I was taught to be strong, to think independently, and to never just believe whatever someone said, especially when it didn't make any sense. This grounding in truth and my strong foundation in Christ allowed me to keep getting up day after day and try again. Many days "getting up" meant waking up, finding something to eat, and binge-watching movies and television, but I kept moving.

This is what it takes to fight against a system that only wants to drug and label

Only the foundation in Christ allowed me to keep fighting.

you. This is what it takes to fight for yourself and your freedom. When you're the only one who knows you're not insane and that you are struggling only because of the nightmares you experienced; you are the only one who can keep that truth alive.

Truth is a very powerful substance. When you know the truth, you can find the strength to keep fighting. I knew the truth of who I was before the shootings, and I also knew that my struggles were the direct result of the shootings. No one could convince me that there was just something wrong with me.

Columbine was the final swing of the axe that severed the tenuous tether to my broken life. I knew that I had been a mess long before the shooting, but afterward I knew I could still see a future that I wanted to pursue. That is what I held on to. I struggled to remember who I was or who I thought I was, and I resisted letting go of the control I thought I needed to survive.

Looking back, I'm amazed at the many ways God made his presence known to me in the midst of the darkness. At times, I thought I was barely maintaining a grip on the line between death and life, but I now understand that I was never as close to death as I assumed. Most of us wish God would physically come down and superglue our broken pieces back together. Better yet that He'd follow the Japanese tradition of Kintsugi and instantly glue our broken pieces together with gold so we would never break again and create a masterpiece in the process.

While this is possible and God truly wants to heal and redeem our worst pain, He also repairs us at the speed required in order for us to grow stronger, develop the ability to shine in the darkness, and restore and redeem our lives fully.

It was the still small voice of God that woke me up in the morning, that whispered, "Don't let go," that pointed my eyes in the direction of the light that I could not find on my own. He is the one who reminded me I still had hopes and dreams, that I was not permanently broken, and that I *would* be able to live again.

We can't create this on our own. The enemy of our souls, Satan, desperately wants to keep us broken, angry, bitter, and destroyed. God wants us to live in freedom, to find the victory over the enemy of our souls, to raise our weary head—swollen from crying ourselves to sleep or awakened from the terror in the night—and see that there is hope.

Choosing to listen to the voice of hope and truth, quietly whispering inside the crevices of your mind, instead of the louder voice of despair and hopelessness, gives you the energy and strength to keep fighting. I am not saying that you just need to have more faith and you will be healed (no seriously, someone *did* tell me that once). I *am* saying, that choosing to believe you can be free, that you can have a different life, is often all that you need to keep trying to find someone or something that can help bring you back to life.

Traveling the perilous roads of healing from trauma is not something you can do on your own. It requires that you find someone trustworthy (likely a professional), again and again, if necessary, to help guide you through what you can't see. The road to healing is not smooth and free of obstacles—in fact, this road is littered with obstacles, fear, loss, and hurt. For this and many other reasons, some people choose to take the fork in the road that circles back to their comfortable prison.

Many people try to navigate this path on their own, relying on their own knowledge and insight of what they think it *should* look like.

"Why don't I feel any different?" a client asked me in one session. "I'm trying, I'm doing everything I can to get better! I don't understand why I still feel this way, why I don't feel like I've changed."

"What do you think you should be feeling now? What are you expecting?"

"For one, I'd like to think that if I was getting any better, I wouldn't be so pissed off all the time. That I'd be sleeping. That I'd want to get up and do anything other than what I'm doing! I don't have the energy to do any of the things I really want to be doing. I expected that would have changed by now."

"It's really hard to see the scope of how we've changed when we focus on everything that isn't the way we want it to be. I see a completely different person sitting in front of me," I told her. "When we first met, there was a raging fire in your eyes desperately trying to hide the fear and chaos behind it. You hadn't slept in weeks, you hadn't showered in just as long, and you'd been on a bender for days before you came in. Now, you sleep every night, even if it doesn't feel like it; you take care of your physical and spiritual needs; and you've been sober for six months. That is the change that you've made. Once you can see that, the rest will follow."

Inevitably, focusing only on what hasn't changed and having unrealistic expectations for the healing process results in hopelessness and frustration.

Nothing is ever the way we think it *should* be. We idealize everything, partly because if it's nice and shiny it won't be so terrifying, and partly because we don't know how else to understand. I learned through my journey that it is unrealistic to believe that coming back from the precipice of death is somehow going to be all sunshine and rainbows. As if clawing your way out of a freshly dug grave would be clean and easy.

Make no mistake about what you are crawling through to finally reach the light and breathe your first breath of clean air since you were buried alive under the pain and suffering. Also make no mistake about the sweet release and freedom that is found when you breach the darkness and take your first deep breath of new life!

The path to true healing and redemption throws open the cell of whatever prison you've been living in and invites you to take small steps out from dark corner and into the light that defeats the darkness. It's messy, painful, sometimes disgusting, offensive, and uncomfortable. So is your existence now. The difference is that when you choose to heal, when you choose the path to freedom, the mess, the pain, and everything else you're living with now, changes and morphs into a memory instead of your reality.

When you fight for yourself and for the help that you need, you not only battle yourself and the demons that relentlessly pursue you, but you also fight against a broken, well-intentioned system that does more harm than good. It is very easy to get discouraged, give up, and try to heal on your own.

The hardest part of this battle, other than deciding to engage it in the first place, is deciding to keep going when no one but you believes the truth.

Choosing to keep fighting for what you know you need, to keep searching for the path that leads you to healing, and to keep taking each step towards the future will get you up out of the grave and bring you back to life.

9

STRENGTH IS FORGED IN THE PAIN

Those who have been traumatized will never be what they were. They are remade into something that is immeasurably stronger, more beautiful, kinder and empathetic.

—Unknown

"It seems like no matter what I do, there are things, moments, that still get to me. Will this ever be different?"

"Things will get better eventually, but you have to redefine what it means to be normal now. Your new normal includes the reality of what you survived. Those scars never totally go away, but they do fade and change. But you can't ever go back to the way it was before. That no longer exists."

When I finally woke up from the cloud of dissociation, nothingness, and destruction that defined my existence for years after the Columbine massacre, I started to resent and became enraged that the life I should have been able to live was snatched away from me and I could do nothing about it. I was incensed and hated everyone and everything and wanted nothing to do with this existence.

I looked at the people in my life fortunate enough to escape the atrocities that plagued me, and I hated them because they were able to laugh freely, love completely, and enjoy life.

Why me? Why did I have to go through this? It's not fair that I am suffering and everyone else seems fine.

What I did not understand at the time is that, according to Dr. Donald Meichenbaum, over the course of a lifetime, 60 percent of people will survive a traumatic event. My suffering blinded me from seeing the suffering other people were enduring at the same time. The concept of resilience—the ability to adapt successfully when experiencing traumatic events—was unfamiliar to me. I didn't see how anyone who experienced something as horrific as I did, could react any differently than me.

I lived for so long with a rageful nothingness in my heart that it created deep and destructive grooves in my mind that produced vengeful thoughts and behavior. The more I reinforced this mind-set and emotional reaction, the clearer that pathway in my mind became. I felt completely cheated out of life and my childhood, and I was livid with everyone and everything.

I deserve better than this! After what I went through, I deserve to have some peace, something different than what I have now.

On some level, I knew my attitude prevented any real change from happening in my life and in my relationships, but I still wanted retribution for what was taken from me.

This struggle between wanting others to pay for what happened to me and the profound and intense longing for a life other than my own caused internal carnage. I tried to exist in both worlds—why shouldn't I demand retribution *and* have a new life? Not until I began to understand the answer was I able to let go.

This battle still continues in my life today, and I understand that I may always struggle with this desire to punish those who hurt other people, but I have learned how to control that part of me that used to be uncontrollable.

I learned that my reaction to the trauma was appro-

Revenge and Life cannot coexist, you must choose.

priate and normal, and it didn't make me a monster. Once I accepted this discovery, I could begin pursuing the new life that would bring my raging mind back under control.

I had to let go of the idea that by forcing people to pay for their actual or perceived attacks, I was somehow going to undo what was done.

I had to let go of the idea that the life I had hoped for, the life that I thought I deserved, and the life that other people seemed to have would somehow be recaptured by emotionally battering myself and other people.

I had to learn to create and accept the new existence, my new normal, one that included nearly unbearable pain and suffering as well as happiness and joy. The new normal contained physical and emotional scars that would never fully disappear. The new normal forced me to choose another career, other relationships, and a reality different than the one I had always imagined myself living.

This is what is required to survive and thrive after traversing the darkest moments of your life. No matter how much I wanted to let go and move forward, I would never be able to do it on my own. We were not designed to handle the pain and suffering in this life on our own. We were created for community, to be surrounded by tribes of people who comfort us while we heal. We were meant to know and rely on God to heal the deep broken places inside of our souls that we can't reach on our own.

I finally realized that for any meaningful change to occur, I would need to change how I interacted with the world. I would need to stop pretending I was strong enough to keep going on my own. The belief that you don't need anyone else to help you, especially God, is borne out of desperate pain and confusion, and is the one lie that damages us the most.

When we see the world as a threat and have no idea who we can and should trust, we instinctually turn inward and make impossible demands on ourselves. The tendency to demand that we should figure out how to survive on our own and the belief that no one will ever truly understand or care about what we're going through and that we are safer and "better" on our own, prevents us from being able to wrap our minds around the truth that our new normal will forever be different than what we used to know.

The first step in finding your new normal is to take a step back and decide who you want to be. This seems like a very simple step, but when you are steeped in trauma and suffering in silence from pain and memories that don't seem to end, you don't know who you *are* anymore, nor do you think about who you want to *be*. You are trying to hold on to the person you used to be instead of imagining the person that you could become.

The earth-shaking truth of surviving trauma is that who you thought you were going to be, those hopes and dreams you had before, will likely morph into something different or completely unrecognizable. You can either reject them or embrace them and heal.

You are now looking at your future and your life through the eyes of someone who, for a moment, truly believed they would have no future, that their life was over. Once you experience that, you will start to question everything, and that will lead you to pursue a new future that would not have been in your view had you not survived what you did. This truth can be difficult to accept, especially if you carefully crafted your future and were looking forward to pursuing that dream. This doesn't mean that you can't still pursue your dream, but success in your future requires you to integrate your traumatic experiences into what you see for your future. You can pretend to pick up where you left off, but you will only be able to do that for so long until you finally break and give in to accepting that you have been forever changed.

When you accept this truth, you can welcome a new future that you never could have foreseen, and willingly bring the experiences from your past into developing a stronger and more potent future. That's when you can truly move forward.

This can also be a very exciting and redemptive season in your life. When you choose to accept that the past is gone and that your life will be different going forward, it opens the possibility for you to start over. Now that you've been through this, you get to choose who you want to be, how you want to live, what you want to change about where you were going, and how you get there.

You begin to plan how you can honor the scars from the past by cultivating a future and an identity that is stronger and more complete than before.

Allowing ourselves to imagine the life we want, to imagine what it will be like when we no longer suffer so deeply, to imagine what it would feel like, what we could accomplish, and who we will be once we have stepped off this path to destruction, activates parts of our brains that are crucial in cultivating hope. Our imagination is an incredibly powerful tool that allows us to shatter the darkness, confusion, and pain, and not just find the light, but create the pathway out of our prison and into true freedom.

10

DISCOVERY OF YOU

A difficult time can be more readily endured if we retain the conviction that our existence holds a purpose—a cause to pursue, a person to love, a goal to achieve.

—John Maxwell

What is the point of fighting then? Why keep going when everything is a battle? What is the purpose?

At this point, you're probably screaming, "But what is the point of fighting? What will I ever gain from this and how can I possibly transform this nightmare into something positive, something in which I can find purpose and meaning?"

This resonates with me in numerous ways, and looking back on my life, is something I've asked repeatedly. Many well-meaning people in my life offered clichés, such as "God doesn't allow pain without a reason" and that He "always has a purpose for the pain we endure." When I was neck deep in the muck of this existence, these comments infuriated me. Mostly because they came from people who had never experienced trauma and had absolutely no idea what they were saying.

The irony is that now I almost understand what their words meant. There's a verse in the Bible that says God counts and stores every tear we cry. I've read that verse hundreds of times, but not until I moved past the point of chaos and into my healing did I truly appreciate what it meant. The comfort and solace found by embracing the truth of those words is profound.

If God counts my tears and stores them for me, it means that He is there, that He knows and feels my pain on an intimate level, and that He cares enough about *me* to pay attention and comfort me in my pain and suffering.

This truth matters because knowing that God values our pain opens our eyes to His greater purpose and creates life-giving meaning out of our suffering.

God is the God of redemption, hope, and healing. If He recognizes and counts my tears, then He can and *will* bring purpose and meaning to this brokenness.

Without acknowledging God's sovereignty (His preeminence) in everything and inviting Him into the places of darkness and brokenness, we can't possibly understand how to change the pain into life. We can spend our lives trying to rationalize away our irrational behaviors, blaming it on trauma. Yet real freedom comes when we channel that pain and suffering into Christ's greater purpose for us.

From an early age, I wanted to be a healer. I knew that I would someday enter the medical field with the hope of focusing on trauma, either in the emergency room or in trauma surgery. Although some might find it disgusting, I wanted to be the first one to see the blood and destruction and then put the broken pieces of that person back together. Blood, gore, and physical trauma never frightened me, and I loved watching reality television shows that showed those kinds of situations firsthand.

Just the thought of saving lives energized me. I wanted to repair damaged people and bring hope to a hopeless situation. As I write this, I'm laughing at the memory of who I thought I was going to be, mostly because now I absolutely do not want to spend eighty hours a week in a job that gives me first-hand experiences of other people's horrific traumas. Turns out that even though I am equipped to compartmentalize that kind of pain and suffering, the healthier I get, the less I am inclined to put myself in those situations.

Most amazing of all is that saving lives, repairing damaged people, and bringing hope into hopeless situations, is exactly what I do today. I do not serve on the front lines of physical trauma, but I do serve on the front lines of psychological and spiritual trauma, in which sometimes God allows me to see how they intersect with physical trauma responses.

I'm doing what I always wanted to do, just in a different venue. One that I much prefer to my original plans. One that I wouldn't have pursued without surviving the Columbine shootings.

Finding and defining purpose and meaning in our lives after trauma requires surrender and trust, which can be difficult.

"What do you mean I have to let go, surrender my hopes and dreams, and trust that something is better?"

"The only way to find who you are now, is by letting go of the control that is destroying your life. You can't be who you were created to be until you let God show you who that is."

Finding and defining purpose and meaning ... requires you to surrender and trust.

Purpose and meaning do not come from a fancy degree, going into debt to pursue your dream, or sitting back and waiting for something to magically appear that fills the void in your soul. In this process you must be willing to change your mind or adjust your expectations.

As children, we hope and dream about the future with bright eyes, heightened expectations, and the courage to do whatever it takes to get there. We can't imagine a life that falls short of our dreams. For many people, these childlike hopes and dreams morph into adult passions and careers.

For others, though, life intervenes, and we allow those beliefs to dissolve into self-doubt, fear, and apathy.

This especially applies to trauma survivors. Believing in a positive hopeful future seems wasteful and pointless.

Hopes, dreams, and goals, however, are essential for figuring out how to transform our pain and suffering into purpose and meaning.

After the shootings I held onto the dream of becoming a medical doctor, so I could help people in their trauma. I kept that dream alive until I realized that I couldn't anymore. I absolutely adore science, especially human anatomy and physiology (the only other class I aced in those first few years apart from psychology). Even though I could barely function and my mind didn't work the way I wanted, I believed I could muscle through anything and still achieve my dreams.

In no way was I going to let the evil that tried to destroy me defeat me and frustrate my plans.

Then I encountered a class I couldn't pass, no matter how many times I tried to retake it (three), or how many tutors or extra credit assignments I completed. In light of the fractured condition of my mind, I simply couldn't grasp the concepts in chemistry.

I am never going to be able to understand this. This is a core class that I can't pass. I'm never going to be a doctor.

The devastation from realizing I wasn't going to reach my goal threw me into a downward spiral. This coincided with the five-year anniversary of the shootings, when my entire carefully crafted world began to unravel, and it almost destroyed me.

In my defeated mind, the evil had won, and I nearly gave up on ever being anything more than a broken "Columbine Survivor." While God in no way created this chaos, He used the hell I was going through, the pain, suffering, loss, and despair, to reframe my understanding of my purpose and where I would derive true meaning in my life.

The hardest part was letting go of what I thought I wanted, so He could lead me to the place I belonged. I would like to tell you that at this point in my evolution, I no longer experienced disappointment and frustration, but that would be totally false.

Ten years after the shootings, I moved across the country and earned my MA in Forensic Psychology to pursue a career in the Federal Bureau of Investigation as a behavioral analyst. In my mind, this absolutely fit me.

God, for some reason, has given me the ability to read people, to understand human behavior in a way that many other people can't. During this time, I made a mental shift from living in other people's traumas as a doctor to becoming a federal agent so I could outsmart, hunt down, and incarcerate the people who cause the trauma. The hilarious irony of this career choice was that I didn't trust law enforcement. They ignored not only the warning signs of impending trauma, but the multitudes of eyewitnesses who saw the third shooter with a gun, in favor of the easier answer. This caused in me deep mistrust of law enforcement, and for years after the shootings, I experienced panic attacks whenever I saw law enforcement.

God, you have a funny sense of humor. I went from being terrified of the police after the shootings to obsessing about becoming a member of the most powerful police force in the country. How ironic.

To this day, I know I would have excelled in that role, had I been able to access it, but God sealed that door in a way I could never open. After my tenth rejection from the FBI, and numerous changes in my personal life, I finally accepted the truth that God did not want me in that role. Again, I wanted to immerse myself in other people's trauma. Maybe I was trying to avoid completing my own healing, or maybe I thought it would be easier than obeying what I believed God wanted me to do.

Not until I married and gave birth to my first son did I completely surrender my life to God. Through this, He led me into doing what I wanted most: bringing hope to the hopeless and providing healing to the lives of the survivors.

The profound shifts in my perspectives, my hopes, my purpose, and my identity, were jarring to say the least. The anger and rage that fueled me in the past contributed to my desire to destroy people who hurt others. If God had allowed me to push open that closed door, I never would have been able to experience the greatest joy and purpose that I have now.

Surrendering who I thought I was and who I wanted to be was physically painful. I remember the palpable pain, nausea, and tightness in my body when I realized I was not going to accomplish those dreams. They were not my destiny, no matter how much I believed they should be. Once I finally embraced my divine call to private practice as a trauma-focused therapist and I took the first step to following that path, the pain and tension released. My body recognized I was now on the path of who I was meant to be and the conflict between what I wanted and what I needed no longer existed.

Understanding and accepting that my traumas comprised *part* of my purpose and meaning in life instead of the deterrent that prevented me from freedom, liberated me in a way I never would have understood before. I'm not saying that God *ordained* suffering in order to form me into the person I am today; but I do believe that God *allowed* the most horrific pain and suffering imaginable to transform me into someone I never would have been without it.

There is always a way to rise from the ashes of who you have become and emerge as someone amazingly beautiful, strong, and complete. You get to spread your wings and open your mind to what is possible.

11

OUT OF THE ASHES,
WE RISE

Life begins on the other side of despair.
—Jean Paul Sartre

"I can't believe it's been almost twenty years."

"Me neither. Some days it feels like it was yesterday. Some days it feels like the shootings never even happened, like just a bad dream that never goes away."

"Somehow we made it. We fought and struggled, but we're okay. We are healthier than many people from school. We are survivors, not victims."

What does it look like to be a survivor who found healing? Like a beautiful, messy life. Nineteen years ago, the summer after my senior year at Columbine High School, the summer after the worst mass shooting in United States history (at the time), I never would have thought that I would be here. Honestly, I never thought I would be anywhere. I was numb, terrified, and rapidly self-destructing, all while preparing to go to college and somehow move forward.

Fighting every day to wake up, get out of bed and do something other than fade into oblivion was exhausting. I had nothing to give anyone, let alone anything to give myself.

I existed, barely.

I felt alone, terrorized, and dead. Rare glimpses of life appeared occasionally, but my pain and the never-ending blackness of my existence quickly overshadowed them.

Living on autopilot became my only means of survival. I managed to graduate from college, live on my own, and hold down jobs. Every day, though, I somehow put one foot in front of the other until I slowly emerged from the darkness and started pursuing the light.

Albeit slowly, intentionally pursuing a life of meaning and purpose, kept me on the path to healing. Looking back, I can acknowledge that the process never ends. Even after you have effectively eradicated the dysfunctional trauma response, the pain, the nightmares, and the flashbacks, something else—a sound, a memory, or an emotion—will remind you that your healing process continues. It's like recovering from cancer. The symptoms are gone and you can't identify any detectable presence of the hell that you once survived, but you know everything could come crashing down again.

When you decide to pursue healing, you understand that the process will continue for the rest of your life. This in no way means you will suffer in torment forever. It just means the invisible wounds hide below the surface. The healing journey creates scarring over what was once a festering, gaping wound, but the wounds never disappear.

Like a multi-layered a cake, you build each layer carefully, covering and steadying the next level on top of the previous one. Each layer must be formed and created the right way to cover the previous one. A miscalculation in centering and leveling the layer can result in the entire cake falling apart at the seams. You do the intense work to ensure that everything holds together in the end. So it is with trauma. Each level of healing covers the previous one but does not remove it.

To build a strong foundation of healing, to keep moving forward, and to pursue a healthy life you need a sturdy infrastructure, which isn't easy. It is strengthened and reinforced by a strong faith and dependence on Christ, developing a strong support network of people, and then allowing them help you fill in the gaps.

Each level of healing is important to build the foundation for your freedom.

Healing is messy, difficult, painful and hard, but worth it.

This far removed from the most significant trauma

in my life, I am still working on myself. Ghosts of that struggle appear when I'm not taking care of myself, when I'm exhausted and overwhelmed, and when I'm caught off guard by something I see or hear. These ghosts of my past will follow me forever, but they no longer have the power to destroy and control me.

Healing for me looks like rarely watching the news and censoring my exposure to social media. It means knowing that I may not ever be okay with my son going to public school, that my experience as a school shooting survivor has left a permanent rift in my conscious of that reality ever being okay, and I don't punish myself for not trying to change that.

My faith in Christ is the only reason I found healing and freedom, and without that foundation, I see no hope for complete healing. I accept that I will, on some level, always struggle around the anniversary of the shooting. As a result of the shooting, I am passionate about being able to defend myself and my family and choose to make responsible, rational choices in that area.

I struggle with accepting my worth and purpose, especially when those deep levels of trauma and pain are unexpectedly or intentionally triggered. While realizing that I still struggle in this area, I also accept that I have not fully healed and that I need to continue working to transform the open wounds into scars.

My amazing family is comprised of survivors. I desperately love them and cannot imagine doing life without them. We trigger each other when we get angry and impatient with each other or are irrational, but we truly love and care for each other. It's a beautiful mess because we have a history, and those invisible wounds are still sensitive and painful when we are not intentional in respecting or acknowledging each other's pain. But I wouldn't want to trade them for anyone else.

God has blessed me with a strong friendship and support network who sustain me when I need them. I know that I can fly out to see my best friend on a whim if I need to. My Mothers of Preschoolers (MOPS) ladies are also available anytime if I need them . . . and I do.

Still, I cry and yell and sometimes lose myself in moments of hurt, disappointment, and fear. I scream at God and ask why. I break down and beg for Him to change my situation. Yet I also know that God holds me when I'm falling apart, when I realize I need to start fighting again. The enemy of my soul who torments me has strengthened my resolve to reach new levels of prayer and spiritual warfare so I can exercise my authority in Christ and make him stop.

I also know that no matter how I feel, a solid foundation will keep me safe. I know that I will come back to center, and that it will be easier this time. I may never fully close all the wounds in my life, but I trust God to be my Comforter and my Redeemer in those moments of brokenness.

Thus far into my healing journey, my life is pretty awesome. Most of the time I feel at peace with who I am, and I love the person I am becoming. God has blessed me beyond my dreams. But I didn't get to this place by sitting back and waiting for someone to intervene. I am here because through every setback, every resurgence of pain, every obstacle and gut-wrenching heartache, I kept fighting. I believe(d) that God was present and actively fighting this battle with me, that I was never alone even when I was by myself. When no one knew the depths of my pain, God comforted me and reassured me that I would be okay. He counted and honored my tears, saving them for the moment when He will use them to heal, and restore everything that was stolen from me.

Wherever you are in your healing, no matter how raw and painful your life feels right now, you always have hope. However, hope doesn't always look like we think it should. It looks like that far away thought that, *maybe someday* . . . Hope looks like opening the door and removing yourself from a destructive situation, even when you have nowhere to go. Hope is getting up Sunday morning and stumbling into church after a weeklong bender and bowing your head asking for help again. Hope looks like calling your partner, asking for forgiveness, and making whatever changes are necessary to fix that broken relationship.

Hope is trying again, when everything seems lost, when you can barely breathe from the pain you are feeling. Hope means never giving up believing that the invisible wounds inside you can someday be healed. Hope is choosing to see tomorrow as a chance for healing and redemption instead of more pain and suffering.

Hope means choosing to pursue a life you can't even begin to see, but you believe could be possible. Surviving the Columbine High School shootings in 1999 temporarily severed my ability to hope, to see beyond the immediate, suffocating pain, and to reach for the light on the other side. I am here today because I never stopped hoping in something. It took many years, a great deal of pain and heartache, many self-destructive choices, and a difficult awakening to begin building boundaries on what that "something" could be.

Hope is choosing to see tomorrow as a chance for healing and redemption.

You don't need to know what the future holds or be able to identify the specifics of your hope. You don't need a clear definition of who you are or what life should be like to pursue healing. You don't need anything beyond the realization that you can hope for something different.

Never give yourself permission to give up the fight. Never stop moving forward, even when you suffer a temporary setback that throws you so far off course you can't see where you were before. Do not allow yourself to succumb to the darkness of trauma and PTSD. You are the only one who can fight your fight, the only one who can win, but you can't do it alone. Choose to seek other people who know what you're struggling with and who have won the battle. Choose to seek help even if you don't yet believe that it will help. Choose to fight the demons in your mind that are trying to convince you that your efforts are hopeless, and you will never be free.

When you choose life, even a messy, difficult path to that life, you have already won half the battle. Once you step on the path to healing and redemption, give yourself permission to stay on it, no matter how difficult and painful it becomes. At the end of the struggle is relief and healing. That is worth any battle you must fight to finally break free and reclaim the life that was stolen from you.

APPENDIX A

DIAGNOSTIC CRITERIA AND SYMPTOMS

The *Diagnostic and Statistical Manual*, Fifth Edition, lists the diagnostic criteria for Posttraumatic Stress Disorder as follows:

A. Exposure to actual or threatened death, serious injury, or sexual violence by either directly witnessing the event, seeing it happen to others, learning of trauma occurring to a close friend or relative, experiencing repeated or extreme exposure to aversive details of the traumatic events (such as in first responders, "helping professions," etc.)

B. Presence of at least one distressing intrusive symptom associated with the traumatic event, such as memories, dreams, dissociative reactions (flashbacks, trauma reenactment in play), extreme distress at internal or external cues (triggers), and marked physiological reactions to triggers (panic, hyperventilation, etc.)

C. Persistent avoidance of stimuli associated with the traumatic event such as actively attempting to avoid memories, thoughts, or feelings related to the trauma and avoidance of external reminders (people, places, objects, activities, etc.)

D. Negative alterations in thinking and mood associated with the traumatic event such as the inability to remember important aspects of the trauma, persistent and exaggerated negative beliefs or expectations about themselves or the world, persistent distorted thoughts about the cause of the consequences of the trauma (blaming themselves, shouldn't have been drinking, been stronger, said no, etc.), persistent negative emotional state (fear, anger, guilt, shame, etc.), marked diminished interest in participation in significant activities, feeling detached or estranged from others, persistent inability to experience positive emotions

E. Marked changes in arousal and reactivity associated with the traumatic event in at least two ways such as irritable or angry outbursts with little or no provocation, reckless or self-destructive behavior, hypervigilance, exaggerated startle response, problems concentrating, sleep disturbances

F. The symptoms must last longer than one month following exposure, cause clinically significant impairment in important areas of life, and not related to a medical condition or substance use (meaning the symptoms predate or are not only present when under the influence)

They go on to specify that these symptoms could also include dissociative symptoms such as depersonalization (persistent or recurrent experiences of feeling detached from their body, as if they were an outside observer of thoughts and behaviors), and de-realization (persistent or recurrent experiences of unreality of surroundings, the world around is unreal, in a dreamlike state, distant, or distorted).

Further, these symptoms can have a delayed expression. This means that some people immediately begin demonstrating symptoms progressing to full diagnostic PTSD and some people may not start experiencing full diagnostic symptoms until at least six months after the event.

Children under the age of six have almost identical criteria, but expression may be different. For example, intrusive memories may appear during play reenactment. They may not be able to identify what is in their nightmares that is causing distress, but the distress is obvious. Dissociative reactions occur on a continuum and often fluctuate. Children often do not have the ability to express what they are experiencing due to their age or age at exposure to trauma, but these symptoms will likely show up in play, art, "bizarre" behaviors, and regression.

Possible co-occurring disorders with PTSD may include other diagnoses in the manual (depression, anxiety, dissociative disorders, personality disorders, obsessive-compulsive disorders, etc.). Paranoia, auditory and visual disturbances, what they term pseudo-hallucinations, can also be present in those with PTSD, especially Complex PTSD. People with PTSD are often misdiagnosed or over-diagnosed with a multitude of labels when a PTSD diagnosis would suffice to capture the scope of suffering.

Exposure to multiple traumas, the severity of the traumas, and the availability of support and safety, affects the probability of developing Complex Posttraumatic Stress Disorder, (C-PTSD). If you have already met the diagnostic criteria for PTSD and experience further trauma, you are more likely to develop new symptoms, or exacerbate and/or reactivate previously experienced symptoms of PTSD.

APPENDIX B

FINDING THE RIGHT TREATMENT FOR YOU

There is not a singular treatment that works for every person who has survived a traumatic event. Some types of treatments may cause further harm or are ineffective with how you process information and trauma. If you are participating in treatment that isn't working, find something that will.

A variety of trauma-focused treatments are available, but I have found some that are more harmful than others. For example, I avoid exposure therapy, which gradually and continually exposes you to the trauma in order to desensitize you and numb you out to any response, in my practice due to the adverse reactions it has caused me and others undergoing this treatment. This is my personal preference, and many people would disagree with me. To help you consider the best treatment for you, I list below a general description of my recommendations.

The more common treatments for PTSD and trauma include forms of cognitive behavioral therapy

(CBT), exposure therapies, and reprocessing therapies. In my practice, I use splankna, emotional freedom technique (EFT), and forms of cognitive behavioral therapy. A brief synopsis of these:

- **Splankna** is a Christian mind-body healing protocol created by Sarah Thiessen and Heather Hughes that is extremely effective at quickly addressing the multiple layers of trauma and bringing healing and freedom to the individual suffering. This technique melds components of EMDR, EFT/TFT (thought field therapy), and NET (neuro-emotive technique), incorporating a biblically sound approach to healing. This combination of mind-body-soul healing, inviting Christ to heal as He promises to do in Scripture, creates the "perfect environment" for healing and, in my experience, achieves freedom much quicker than traditional methods.

- **Emotional Freedom Technique (EFT) or Thought Field Therapy (TFT)** was developed by Dr. Roger Callahan, this therapeutic technique uses tapping sequences, where the person physically taps on energy meridian points while repeating specific phrases about their symptoms or their trauma. Sherrie Rice Smith added to this technique the implementation of biblically sound theology which enhances this tool by bringing the truth of Christ's sovereignty into the healing process.

- **Cognitive Behavioral Therapy (CBT)** was developed by Aaron Beck, utilizes tools and techniques to illuminate and address cognitive distortions and errors in thinking that contribute to ongoing, unwanted symptoms. CBT can be extremely effective in helping identify patterns of thoughts that contributing to your struggles. Engaging in this treatment and using these tools will create change over time.

- **Cognitive Processing Therapy (CPT)** focuses on the connections between thoughts, feelings, behavior, and bodily sensations. According to the creator of this treatment, Patricia A. Resick, CPT provides a way to understand why recovery from traumatic events is difficult and how symptoms of PTSD affect daily life. The focus is on identifying how traumatic experiences change thoughts and beliefs, and how thoughts influence current feelings and behaviors.

• **Systematic Desensitization, and Eye-Movement Desensitization and Reprocessing (EMDR)**, created by Francine Shapiro, is a psychotherapy that enables people to heal from the symptoms and emotional distress that result from disturbing life experiences. This treatment utilizes rapid eye movement and other bilateral brain stimulation to help the mind reprocess traumatic events and allows the person to move beyond the trauma.

Many other options for addressing trauma and PTSD are available, however, the ones I listed have been shown to be consistently effective in treating traumatized people. When you search for the right treatment, keep the following in mind:

Here are some tips to help you know if you're receiving the right treatment:

A. You will feel safe during treatment. If the provider or proposed course and type of treatment results in feelings of fear, anxiety, or other unbearable/harmful responses, then you are not going to find relief.

B. You will begin to feel different and better as a result of the treatment. Six months into treatment, if nothing has changed and you are not moving forward in any area of healing (and this is echoed by your provider and those in your life), then the treatment is not right for you.

C. If at any point the provider begins "suggesting" what may have happened, questioning your memory, minimizing what your experiencing, or pressuring you into doing something that you are not comfortable with, then find someone who will listen, be patient, ethical, and appropriate while walking alongside you as you heal.

*Note of clarity here: Because trauma impacts a person's ability to effectively understand what is happening and what is real, the provider is responsible for helping you see the blind spots and destructive behavior patterns you have developed in response to the trauma. This is never comfortable. You will likely be upset at some things your counselor asked you to consider. Trauma victims often make destructive choices because that's where they feel safe. But your counselor may ask you to consider those choices, and that line of questioning may result in intense emotional reactions. I found my counselor's words made me angry until I processed them on my own and realized what she was really saying or asking me to do.

Traumatized people are exceptionally skilled at self-protection and often develop walls and patterns of behavior for a reason. Any trauma-informed provider worth seeing will challenge you to change that. Expect it to be uncomfortable.

A provider should *never* do the following:

A. Make sexual advances or crude jokes or innuendos

B. Ignore and dismiss your symptoms

C. Ask you to do something illegal, immoral, or unethical

D. Ask you for favors, quid pro quo, or special treatment or discounts if you provide a service of some sort as a business

E. Ignore your concerns, refuse to answer your questions about the treatment offered (for example: Why this treatment? What should I expect? How does it work? Why will it work? Are you trained or knowledgeable?)

F. Suggest a different reality than what you are describing as a means of explaining your symptoms (for example: maybe you ask why you can't work out like you want to and the counselor suggests you were sexually abused as a child, which resulted in believing that your physical body is broken, which is why you don't want to run)

APPENDIX C

RESOURCES

IF YOU ARE SUICIDAL DIAL 911. There is no shame in asking for help, and the demons and lies that are infiltrating your mind telling you that death is the only way out, will only be stopped by proclaiming the truth and getting help. Don't give up the fight because your mind tells you that you have no hope.

IF YOU ARE IN A LIFE-THREATENING DOMESTIC VIOLENCE SITUATION and don't know who to reach out to, call the National Domestic Violence hotline and they will help you: **1-800-799-7233.**

Websites
- http://InvisibleWoundsllc.org
- https://splankna.com/
- https://cptforptsd.com/
- http://www.emdr.com/
- https://eftforchristians.com/
- https://beckinstitute.org/

- http://www.thehotline.org/
- https://www.istss.org/   (International Society for Traumatic Stress Studies)
- https://www.ptsd.va.gov

Books

The Body Keeps the Score: Brain, Mind, and Body in the Healing of Trauma by *Bessel van der Kolk*

Switch on Your Brain: The Key to Peak Happiness, Thinking, and Health by *Dr. Caroline Leaf*

Finding the UPside of Down: How Tragedy Can Lead to Remarkable and Dramatic Breakthroughs by *Lucille Zimmerman*

Waking the Tiger: Healing Trauma by *Peter A. Levine*

Splankna: The Redemption of Energy Healing for the Kingdom of God by *Sarah J. Thiessen*

Upperdogs: Christians Have the Advantage. It's Time to Take it by *Heather Hughes* and *Sarah Thiessen*

CPSIA information can be obtained
at www.ICGtesting.com
Printed in the USA
LVHW112247080219
606878LV00005BA/8/P